primary RECORDS *of* ACHIEVEMENT

A TEACHERS' GUIDE TO REVIEWING, RECORDING AND REPORTING

primary RECORDS — *of* — ACHIEVEMENT

A TEACHERS' GUIDE TO REVIEWING, RECORDING AND REPORTING

Gillian Johnson, Barry Hill and Pat Tunstall
London Record of Achievement Team,
Institute of Education, University of London

Hodder & Stoughton

A MEMBER OF THE HODDER HEADLINE GROUP

The authors

Gillian Johnson joined the London Record of Achievement Team in January 1991 after working with CATS Key Stage 1 developing materials for SAT assessment. She has substantial primary teaching experience and has also worked as a primary advisory teacher with the ILEA. She has written a number of books and articles on assessment.

Barry Hill was appointed as Assessment Officer within the London Record of Achievement Team in April 1990. An experienced teacher, he was previously a Development Officer with ILEA's Central Assessment Team and worked with schools to support practice in recording achievement. He has contributed to a range of guidance materials produced by the London Record of Achievement Team.

Pat Tunstall became Director of the London Record of Achievement Scheme when it was established in April 1990 at the Institute of Education. Previously, she was an Assessment Co-ordinator with ILEA's Central Assessment Team and was involved in development work for records of achievement with a number of primary schools. By background a teacher, she has experience in primary, secondary and higher education. She has contributed to several publications as well as written guidance materials.

ISBN 0 340 57329 5

First published 1992
Impression number   10 9 8 7 6 5 4
Year   1998 1997 1996 1995 1994

Typeset by Wearset, Boldon, Tyne and Wear.

Printed in Great Britain for Hodder & Stoughton Educational, a division of Hodder Headline Plc, Mill Road, Dunton Green, Sevenoaks, Kent TN13 2YA by The Bath Press, Bath, Avon.

Foreword

How best to keep records on pupils' progress is a challenge to primary teachers. Given that individuals both learn in different ways, and make progress at different speeds, the task can so easily expand until it is quite impossible to manage alongside the many other demands on a teacher's time. Jean Piaget, who was a pioneer in the recording of children's intellectual progress, only had to cope with his own children: a modern primary teacher may have to cope with a class of 30. Charting developments – intellectual, personal and social – is, however, a fascinating activity, as many teachers have also discovered.

Primary Records of Achievement has been developed in order to help teachers manage this task. Drawing on the principles that have been developed over the last ten or so years by those working with various forms of pupil records, and learning from their experiences, the London Record of Achievement team at the Institute of Education has sought to create a tool that suits primary schools. They have avoided producing a hand-me-down from secondary practice and have created something based on primary class experience which fits the National Curriculum recording and reporting arrangements into a framework of development suitable for the whole child.

This important work has been made possible by the existence of a consortium of London Local Education Authorities (Camden, Greenwich, Hammersmith and Fulham, Hackney, Islington, Lambeth, Lewisham, Southwark, Waltham Forest and City of Westminster) and the Institute of Education, University of London. This Consortium has supported the team at the Institute in order to enable the work of the London Record of Achievement to continue within the broad remit of developing the recording and reporting of achievement across all phases of education. The guide is a tribute to the commitment of the Local Education Authorities involved and to their partnership with the Institute of Education.

A feature of this guide is its wide use of examples of practice from primary schools. Thanks are due to those teachers, pupils and schools who have given permission for their examples to be included. Particular thanks are also due to members of the London Record of Achievement Steering Committee for their support; to the Primary Working Group chaired by Barbara MacGilchrist in which ideas about guidance material were generated; to the London Record of Achievement team itself for undertaking the work, namely Gillian Johnson who undertook the main body of the writing, Barry Hill and Pat Tunstall.

With the requirements of the National Curriculum changing primary practice, it is essential that teachers have a broad framework for recording and reporting in which the statutory requirements can be met while incorporating the important processes of involving pupils and parents in recording achievement. I hope this guide will be of value to primary teachers in developing effective classroom practice.

Professor Peter Mortimore
Institute of Education, University of London

Contents

Introduction

Primary Records of Achievement: a teachers' guide to reviewing, recording and reporting aims to provide you as the teacher with a whole perspective on recording and reporting. In these areas, the guide gets to the heart of the issues by relating them to the processes of recognising and building upon achievement.

Creating a record of achievement is an approach which encourages children to take responsibility for their own learning. The guide shows how good primary practice can be developed within a framework which also allows teachers to manage the statutory requirements of the National Curriculum. The important but informal aspects of assessment, recording and reporting, such as children keeping their own log books of group work, are shown to be essential elements of formative recording and a support for curriculum management. These are easily overlooked with the present anxieties about recording statements of attainment.

The guide does not provide a format for recording or suggest replacement of your existing recording systems. We recognise that schools and local education authorities have already given much thought to the design of formats for teacher records and reports. Rather the emphasis in the guide is on the processes and practice of recording achievement.

Time is one of the biggest factors to be reckoned with in recording achievement; this guide also provides some discussion of the ways teachers are organising and managing their classrooms to allow time for creating records of achievement.

The discussion within the chapters is informed by the practical experience of primary classrooms and we are very grateful to the many primary teachers who have allowed us to use examples of their records.

We hope this guide works for you.

Acknowledgements

We should like to thank the following schools, which kindly allowed us to reproduce examples of children's work:

Archbishop Michael Ramsey CE Secondary School, Southwark
Ashmole Primary School, Lambeth
Beckford Primary School, Camden
Henry Fawcett Primary School, Lambeth
Lilian Baylis Secondary School, Lambeth
Lyndhurst Primary School, Southwark
Peckham Park Primary School, Southwark
St George's CE Primary School, Southwark
St Winifred's RC Infant School, Lewisham
St Winifred's RC Junior School, Lewisham

We should also like to thank Ann Neesom and Daya Moodley for their assistance in collecting examples of practice.

Detailed acknowledgements are provided in the text to the Centre for Language in Primary Education, the Department of Education and Science, Hammersmith and Fulham LEA, and the South London Science and Technology Centre, for allowing us to reproduce extracts from the records and documents they have produced.

We should like to thank members of the inspectorate and advisory teachers from the LEAs within the London Record of Achievement Scheme for their interest and support throughout the development of this guide.

We are very grateful to the administrative and secretarial staff of the London Record of Achievement Team, Peter Giffin and Carol Murray, for all their help in producing this book.

SECTION ONE

Setting the Scene

This section looks at the important principles that underlie the processes of recording achievement; it focuses on achievement itself as an approach to assessing, recording and reporting individual children's progress and development. The framework for recording achievement provides a picture of the different elements and the way in which these are linked together. It enables teachers to see how their present recording formats might be used in working with children to create their own records of achievement.

1
Principles and purposes of recording achievement

In considering the principles upon which records of achievement are based, it is important to be clear about the term 'achievement' and ways in which this differs from 'attainment'.

Attainment is concerned with *mastery* against defined criteria. Within the National Curriculum children's progress must be graded against specific criteria for attainment. Children are required to demonstrate that they can do the things specified within the 'statements of attainment'.

To master, to successfully attain, is an important aspect of achievement. But achievement is broader than attainment in many respects.

First, progress represents achievement, even where this does not encompass complete mastery. Vygotsky has talked of the 'zone of proximal development', the importance of recognising what children can do *with a degree of help*. With a teacher's assistance through prompting, supporting, encouraging, children may be able, for example, to organise their thinking sufficiently to 'Add and subtract using a small number of objects' (Ma2/1b) while they are yet unable to do such a calculation by themselves. For individual children this might represent real achievement, but could not properly count as *attainment* because of the teacher's intervention.

Children frequently demonstrate, unaided, *partial* mastery of a skill or a concept. In developing a concept of number to ten, for example, a child may be able to read numbers from zero to ten but not be able to write or order the numbers. While such a child cannot be said to have attained complete mastery of the concept in terms of the National Curriculum criterion, teachers will be able to identify areas of progress and achievement.

Mastery itself implies that children are able to attain against a specific criterion *in any context*. Achievement, on the other hand, can be acknowledged in any circumstance where children show capability, even though teachers are aware of, and document, the limited contexts in which children demonstrate what they can do.

Secondly, there are qualities crucial to children's *ability* to attain which cannot be talked about in terms of mastery but only in terms of continuing personal development. For example, qualities such as persistence, self confidence and ambition in different areas are not mastered but build up gradually and can only be discussed in terms of continuing progress and achievement. Children who remain on task in any area they find challenging are achieving, and this can be recognised even if their efforts will not result in mastery of a new skill for some time.

The principles which underlie primary records of achievement use the definition of achievement in the widest sense. They are founded on the importance of recognising children's needs as individual learners and of building on their achievements.

This means that primary records of achievement:

- recognise achievement in all its aspects: across the curriculum as a whole, in personal and social areas, within the life of the school and outside school, so providing a rounded picture of a child's achievement;
- help children to build on strengths, recognise needs and overcome weaknesses in their work, thus contributing to children's motivation and personal development;
- are based on the processes of reviewing and on-going recording which involve children in recognising progress and planning future learning;
- provide opportunities for parents to become involved;
- support continuity of progress when children change classes or schools;
- provide a framework within which schools can use assessment formatively and evaluate their curriculum planning and recording.

The aim of this guide is to show, in practical ways, how these principles and purposes can be supported in the primary classroom.

2
A framework for recording achievement

Recording achievement in the classroom involves children and teachers in the process of:

- deciding on the criteria for achievement
- finding appropriate ways of recording
- collecting work
- selecting work
- reviewing
- setting targets.

The evidence of achievement takes many forms and can appropriately be organised within:

- **the child's portfolio of work**
  This contains the day-to-day evidence of classroom achievement as well as evidence of achievement in all parts of school life and outside school; the responsibility for managing this portfolio is with the child.
- **the teacher's profile folder**
  This contains the child's profiles and reports as well as work samples showing the child's progress; the teacher maintains this part of the record of achievement and selects from it appropriate documents to forward to the next teacher. At the end of Year 6, or whenever the child changes school, the profile folder passes to the secondary school as part of the official record of achievement for the child.
- **the child's personal record of achievement**
  The personal record of achievement can be a straightforward selection of evidence of achievement from the portfolio that the child wants to take forward into the next class. In Year 6, or whenever the child changes schools, this personal record can also include a statement by the child that summarises primary school achievement. The record belongs to the child

The child's portfolio

This has work samples and evidence of achievement collected by the child. Within the portfolio the child may wish to include:

- written work
- project work, photographs or drawings of models
- photocopies of work from books or work from home
- photocopies of certificates and awards
- maps, diagrams and plans
- drawings and paintings
- audiotape or videotape recordings
- diaries and work logs.

With all work samples and evidence, it is useful to have a note by the child or teacher explaining the context.

At the end of each year the child takes the portfolio home.

The teacher's profile folder

This folder is a record of individual achievement and progress written and retained by the teacher which includes some of the following:

- work samples from the child's portfolio, chosen by the child and teacher and annotated by the teacher
- notes of teacher–child reviews with agreed targets
- recorded classroom observations
- diaries, descriptions, accounts, Primary Language or Learning Record
- records of conferences with the child
- records of parent–teacher discussions
- home to school information from parents
- teacher record sheets, graphs, charts and computer aided records
- a copy of the annual report to parents
- National Curriculum attainment target levels.

The formative review process

The contents of the portfolio and profile folder are reviewed by the teacher and child. An agreed selection of work samples from the portfolio is transferred into the profile folder.

The child and teacher agree the notes that are taken to:

- show progress and achievement
- identify needs
- outline targets.

The end-of-year summative review process

The focus of this review between the child and teacher can be:

- the contents of the profile folder
- self-assessments provided by the child, eg for Primary Language or Learning Record
- work samples, with some being put into the teacher's annual summary record and others retained in the child's portfolio

The outcomes of this review provide the basis for the teacher's annual report to parents.

Figure 1 *An annual framework for recording children's achievement through primary school.*

The annual portfolio collection retained by the child

The child takes this record with him/her from class to class. Documents included in this record are:

- chosen work samples
- evidence of school achievement beyond the curriculum
- evidence of achievement outside school.

The child's summary record of achievement presented at the end of primary school

This record is owned by the child who uses it when moving into secondary school. Documents included in this record are:

- the child's personal statement of achievement
- chosen work samples
- evidence of school achievement beyond the curriculum
- evidence of achievement outside school.

For children

Reports to parents

Annual report

End of Key Stage report

For parents

The teacher's annual summary record of achievement

Documents are selected from the profile folder which reflect the child's achievements through the year. These documents may include:

- relevant teacher's notes
- LEA/school summative record sheet
- end of year reports for parents
- significant work samples.

The teacher's summary record of achievement at transfer

Documents are selected from the profile folder which reflect the child's achievements through the primary phase. These documents can include:

- relevant teacher's notes
- LEA or school summative record sheet
- end of year reports for parents
- end of Key Stage records of attainment target levels
- significant work samples.

For teachers

and some schools use a presentation folder to underline ownership, celebrate achievement and encourage continued use of the record in secondary schools.

Whenever a child changes school the teacher's profile folder and the child's personal record of achievement form the summary documents that can be used by the new school. Where children change schools between Years 6 and 7, summary documents are compiled during Year 6. However, where the organisation of schooling is different, as for example with Years 5 to 9 middle schools and some special schools, these summary documents are needed in other years.

How the processes and outcomes of recording achievement relate to each other are shown in Figure 1.

Confidential records

Separate from the documents that detail and summarise a child's achievement are the confidential records kept by the school, often on computer. These records include family details, emergency telephone number and medical records, and are transferred to a child's new school.

SECTION TWO

Processes of Review and Assessment

This section describes the classroom practice fundamental to the recognition and recording of achievement. Detailed consideration is given to the central role of children in the processes of assessment and the practical ways in which they become involved through review, self-assessment and selection of work for the portfolio.

3
Conducting reviews

This chapter describes the most important process in the creation of a record of achievement: the organisation and conduct of reviews. A review is a special time set aside for individual children to talk privately with their teacher about their achievements, hopes and concerns. The discussion focuses on progress and achievements since the last review. A child's concerns are acknowledged and discussed in a constructive, forward-looking way.

The items in the child's portfolio should illustrate a broad range of achievement, and will form the basis for the review discussion. In the course of this discussion evidence of achievement is selected by both child and teacher and transferred from the portfolio to the on-going teacher's records in the profile folder. This sampling process itself is important. There are a number of different criteria which need to be taken into account and the process of selection is dealt with in more detail in Chapter 5.

The notes and observations you have collected in your own teacher's profile folder since the last review can be shared with the child. Sharing your own records on progress emphasises the child's status as a partner and supports the integrity of the review process.

Through the review discussion each child can be helped to see more clearly what the next steps in learning should be, and can agree the targets for learning. These are written down and kept in the profile folder; in some schools there is a pro-forma, as shown in the example on page 16, for recording targets. They provide a very good focus for your curriculum planning for the child and the degree to which the agreed targets have been met should be a part of the next review session.

With all children, the review process provides an opportunity for you to:

- reinforce a sense of achievement across a range of activities and interests;
- establish their needs, and give the sense that these needs are understood and supported in ways they can recognise and understand;
- develop in them a more confident sense of themselves as learners and increase their control of the learning process;
- focus their attention on the next steps in their learning by agreeing and setting targets;
- ensure that assessment is used formatively in curriculum planning.

Finding time to review

Finding significant amounts of time in which to conduct reviews has been a major concern for teachers. Most have found it necessary to adopt a systematic approach to managing reviews.

Daily reviews

Some teachers set aside five or ten minutes at the same time each day, say, immediately after lunch, for a review session with one or two children. They feel that this establishes the review as a familiar part of the day when children know that most of them will need to work independently for a short time, perhaps reading quietly. Although the review time is short it enables the teacher to establish the importance of reviews as a regular part of classroom practice.

Weekly reviews

In some cases the review sessions are seen as sufficiently important to set aside one afternoon each week, and to review progress with one group of children on a rota basis. The reviews can then have a significant impact upon the teacher's on-going records.

Termly reviews

Other teachers prefer to arrange reviews, of about fifteen minutes for each child, around curricular activities. This usually means that teachers conduct a review with each child once in a term.

Making preparations

Reviews offer excellent opportunities for you to help children move forward in their thinking, but there is a delicate balance to be struck between stimulating and directing them. In preparing for reviews it is important to think through ways in which this balance can be created as you raise issues with the child and establish a supportive ethos for the review. Good preparations also enable time to be used most effectively.

It is helpful if you have already looked through the work samples before the review begins and have identified the areas where a child has made special progress or broken new ground. This helps to ensure from the outset that the focus is on achievement. Although identifying needs is an important part of every child's review, it is essential that the discussion does not centre on the child's failings. Needs can be identified very successfully when, after a positive review of what the child is currently able to do, you plan together the next steps forward.

It is important that teachers do not monopolise reviews and that children feel a degree of control over the process. However, some forward planning may be necessary to get a dialogue started. Very young children and those inexperienced in reviews often find it difficult to reflect on what they have done and to think ahead. Some careful leading may be unavoidable and this is likely to be most natural and effective if teachers are well prepared.

Supporting bilingual children

In preparing for reviews with bilingual children you may wish to involve a mother tongue teacher, where this is possible. If this support is not available, careful planning may enable you to conduct at least part of a review with children who are not fluent in English.

In some class activities teachers use children fluent in English, who share another child's mother tongue, as translators. However this is not necessarily appropriate for reviews, where children are being invited to talk quite personally.

One way in which bilingual children might help friends who are not fluent in English is by describing to them their own reviews. The organisation of the review, and the process of choosing favourite work samples, could be explained in mother tongue. It might then be possible for the teacher to review the portfolio using language and gesture, so giving a child who is not sufficiently fluent in English some access, albeit limited, to the review process.

Choosing where to hold the review

You will need to choose a quiet area for the review. Here you can talk privately with the child, and items from the portfolio together with notes from the profile folder can be spread out and discussed. The spatial relationship between you and the child is important, and discussion may be more relaxed if you sit side by side rather than facing each other. A feeling of partnership will be fostered more effectively if you are both seated at similar levels.

Carrying out the review

A good way to start the review is by talking about an area of the curriculum which the child particularly enjoys, or a piece of work which is seen as pleasing, especially if some aspect of this work has been shared with the class. You can encourage the child to describe how the work arose, how it was completed, what help was needed and used, and what feelings the child has about the outcome.

Out-of-school activities can also provide a starting point. Some children may be encouraged to participate and feel that they have greater control of the discussion in areas where they know more than the teacher. Information supplied by parents, for example at open evenings, can be useful in identifying these areas and avoiding inappropriate or sensitive issues.

Children should see the review as a time when they have a leading role, rather than a question and answer session led by the teacher. Nevertheless, in preparing for the review you might decide to have questions or ideas at hand to get this discussion started. Some staff have together devised quite detailed 'prompt sheets', of the kind illustrated in Figure 2, as part of their whole-school policy.

If you feel this is too formal, you might prefer simply to note down a few open questions. For example, when looking at a child's writing you might ask:

- Do you enjoy writing?
- If you can choose to do anything, do you sometimes choose to write?
- Which are your favourite pieces of writing?
- Did you share them with friends, the class or your family?
- What did they say about them?
- Do you prefer to write on your own or with friends?
- Who do you enjoy working with? Why?
- What was easy and hard to do in a particular piece of work, for example getting the ideas, writing them down, spelling punctuation?
- Is there any project work you would really like to do that you have not been able to do yet?
- Is there anything that you are not sure about, or would like help with?

Once a child begins to talk it is often more informative to follow her or his train of thought and encourage ideas to be developed, even if these are not quite what you expected or intended. This can lead to frank comments by the child and

```
                    REVIEWS : SOME REMINDERS

MAKE ACHIEVEMENT THE FOCUS

Be positive about what the child can do.

Keep in mind a wide range of achievement.

Remember that taking part can be an achievement.

THINGS TO LOOK FOR

(N.B. this is a reminder of possible areas for discussion,
some of which may be appropriate for a particular child, not
a list of areas to be covered).

Personal and social achievements: examples

        Can take responsibility (own work/class activities)
        Shows awareness of and concern for others
        Can work constructively with others
        Can persist when work is difficult
        Enjoys wide range of activities, will try new things.

In-school achievements: examples

        Development in curriculum areas
            Progress within areas
            New areas of work begun
            Evidence of attainment within N.C.
        Participation in school events, clubs and
            societies
        Activities which recognise child's first language.

Out of school achievements: examples

        Interests, pursuits
            (reading, collections, computers, penfriends)
        Membership of clubs,eg Beavers, Cubs, Guides
        Membership of church organisations, choirs
        Social and cultural achievements within
            community groups
        Voluntary work,eg sponsorship, Blue Peter appeals
        Skills,eg musical achievements, dancing, angling,
            computer skills, athletics, sports.

DEVELOPMENT

What does he/she feel good about, proud of?

What would he/she like to be able to do, or improve?

What support would help?
```

Figure 2 *Some teachers find it useful to have this kind of a prompt sheet to hand when they begin to conduct reviews with children.*

insights into feelings and attitudes which never arise in a 'question and answer' session where, it is widely acknowledged, the child's attention usually focuses on guessing what is in the teacher's mind.

The way in which issues are raised with the child is very important. Closed questions, such as *'Do you think your maths work has improved?'*, are likely to lead to 'Yes' or 'No' answers and are unlikely to help the child to reflect. When framing more open questions it is also important to consider the demands they make on a young child's language and powers of reasoning. *'Why do you think your maths work has improved?'* is clearly a more open question, but answering it requires the manipulation of very sophisticated concepts and language skills which might well tax an adult.

Agreeing targets

A better way to introduce ideas of development with a young child might be to talk more generally about how an activity was done. By referring back directly to notes of previous reviews, you can point out to the child differences in her or his response. Using annotated work samples, you can also talk about the different kinds of help that the child has needed and used. An older child might be encouraged to focus on achievements in different areas. The child can compare feelings of confidence and enjoyment in each of these areas and the ways in which the work was undertaken.

As children begin to reflect on what they would like to be able to do, what they think they are good at and what kinds of help they have needed, this gives you the basis for considering in a practical way how each child's work in class might be improved and the support needed to bring this about. These

---

Record of a review between:

_____ **and** _____
(child)   (teacher)

on _____
         (date)

Achievements

For example, things to be
pleased about; things done
well; improvements

What/who has helped?

Agreed plans and targets

For example, new things to
try; things to improve

Help needed

Signed _____   Signed _____
            (child)   (teacher)

Figure 3 *One example of the kind of format schools are developing for recording the outcomes of reviews.*

considerations are formalised in the setting and writing down of agreed targets. In turn, these feed into your curriculum planning and provide a baseline for the next review with the child. Teachers are developing their own approaches, but in beginning to review with children it may be helpful to focus on two or three areas at most for target setting.

Evaluating your role

Some possible ways to evaluate

Fostering children's self awareness and ability to discuss work is a very skilled process. You may find it useful to evaluate the review discussions by, for example, tape recording a review and listening objectively to your interaction with a child or observing review sessions held by colleagues.

Some questions to be asked

You might then consider:

- How appropriate was the setting for the review? Was the child at ease?
- Who did most of the talking?
- How often was the initiative in the discussion taken by the child?
- What was the quality of the child's reflection on herself or himself as a learner?
- How have you or your colleagues supported reflection by the child during the discussion?
- How confident was the child in discussing new targets?
- How wide ranging was the discussion? Did it include particular talents, extra-curricular activities and interests?
- Were the outcomes useful for forward planning?
- What classroom activities would develop the child's confidence and understanding?

Planning for time

Planning for time to conduct reviews and to evaluate their effectiveness will form an important part of any whole-school policy on assessment and record-keeping based upon primary records of achievement. Suggestions for the ways in which staff might set about developing such a policy are discussed in Chapter 9.

4
Helping children to assess their own achievements

Children need to understand and assess their own progress if they are to contribute effectively to reviews, and to have a voice in forward planning.

The ability to recognise and value achievement is part of children's all-round development. It can help build self-esteem and motivation, and add to children's sense of control of their own learning. As children become more selective and analytical, self-assessment supports cognitive development by encouraging them to become reflective and consider reasons, causes and effects.

Developing an awareness of achievement

Encouraging a focus on achievement

Self-assessment is challenging for children of all ages. The youngest children will need to develop a concept of 'achievement' on which they can build. Gradually they can be helped to reflect upon their own skills, understanding and personal qualities in a balanced, analytical way. Self-assessment can be fostered from the time children enter school, and a good way for teachers to begin with young children is by helping them to focus upon their own and others' achievements.

You can encourage children to focus on achievement by, for example, asking them to:

- bring news of out-of-school interests, activities and awards to share with classmates;
- write down achievements, both in and out of school, and add them to a class display;
- collect together evidence and make individual pictorial records of their achievements;

Figure 4 *Home-to-school liaison: some schools have home-to-school booklets which, as well as providing parents with information, invite them to contribute information on their children's pre-school interests and development. Often, parts of these booklets are designed for parents and children to read and complete together, as in the example. Items like this, which focus on different areas of personal achievement, could be used to open a child's portfolio.*

- present work to the class; show models or drawings, read stories aloud;
- demonstrate skills in areas such as physical education or music.

Encouraging support from parents

Parents can play an on-going part in recognising achievement by encouraging their children to talk reflectively about out of school activities and to bring to school certificates and materials which can be shared with the class.

Promoting a supportive class ethos

The development of children's ability to recognise and share achievements depends upon the ethos of the class and the sensitivity of children to the need in others for recognition and praise. A supportive ethos can be promoted by encouraging children to look at each other in positive ways. This increases their ability to reflect on issues and creates the classroom conditions in which they have the confidence to assess themselves.

Schools such as Henley Primary School have recognised the importance of positive attitudes to peers and the SEAC report

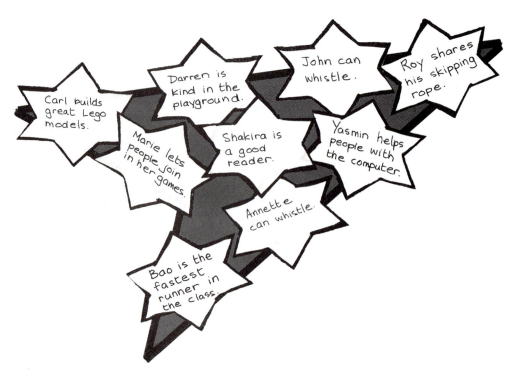

Figure 5 *Part of a class display showing young children's positive comments on their peers. Every child was included.*

on their work shows how they actively promote this in the classroom:

'With children in Year R, each child says something positive about every other child and this is the beginning of developing a positive and caring attitude to each other. With Years 2 and 3, the teacher has organised discussion in groups, looking for good points and avoiding negative attitudes.'

(*Records of Achievement in Primary Schools*, SEAC, 1990, page 56.)

These kinds of activities develop a positive and supportive class ethos. Children can gradually feel safe enough to talk and share ideas, confident that these will be accepted. This provides a basis for the development of paired and group activities in which children begin to discuss their own and others' work in a critical yet constructive way. Self-assessment taking place within a review of a child's achievement then becomes a meaningful, natural extension of class life.

Making presentations

Presentations and demonstrations provide opportunities for the recognition of achievement, and for reflection and self-assessment. They are also important components of National Curriculum work. For example, children's development in technology is assessed through presenting ideas:

'describe to others how they are going about their work'

and by demonstrating skills:

'show that they can use simple hand tools, materials and components'

(Technology AT3, Level 2.)

For all children, and particularly those with special educational needs, it is important that presentations to an audience are founded on a child's strengths. Care needs to be taken to ensure that all children have an equal opportunity to be included. Comparisons between children should be made in a constructive and supportive way, without causing feelings of inadequacy in any children.

You may need to advise on the choice of work to be presented or publicly demonstrated, and encourage the child to rehearse a presentation. Some children may need plenty of opportunities to be part of a group when presenting or demonstrating work to the whole class.

Supporting bilingual children

It is particularly important to ensure that children for whom English is a second language are given support which enables them to take part in presentations. You may want to include activities which are not heavily dependent upon spoken language. With careful organisation, presentations can also provide excellent opportunities for children to demonstrate bilingual skills.

Encouraging children to become reflective

Even the youngest children can be encouraged to reflect on things they have done, and at first their thinking may centre on things they like or dislike. Children have opinions on a wide variety of topics, and are usually happy to explain them, as Figure 6 shows:

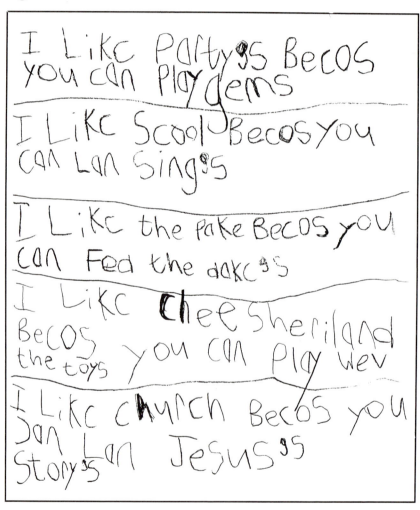

Figure 6 *This Year 1 child not only listed a range of things he liked, but also explained the reasons for his choice.*

As children's confidence and self-esteem grows, they need to be encouraged to talk about their feelings and ideas, as shown in Figure 7. This is a first step towards becoming more deeply reflective and analytical.

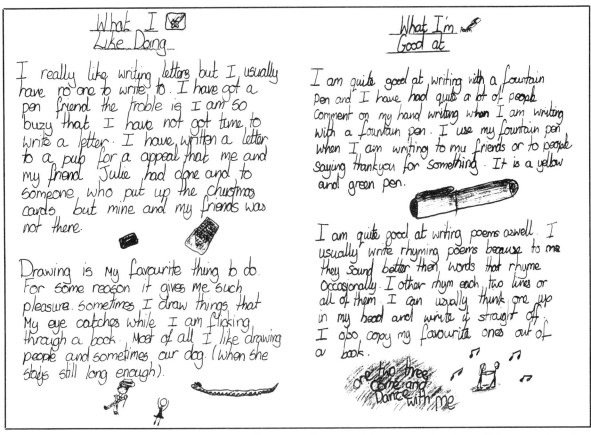

Figure 7 *Comment from an older child (Year 6) on things she likes to do and things she believes she is good at.*

Curriculum planning can include activities which promote reflection sensitively yet effectively by:

- **carefully selecting stories and poetry dealing with children's feelings to be read and discussed in class**
  Children often identify closely with the feelings of characters in stories. Books like *Angry Arthur* (Hiawyn Oram), and *Where the Wild Things Are* (Maurice Sendak) deal with powerful emotions and provide a safe avenue through which these emotions can be explored. For older children, books like *The Trouble with Donovan Croft* (Bernard Ashley) explore feelings and behaviour within social contexts familiar to many children.
- **providing opportunities for drama and role-play**
  A rich variety of opportunities exist, from the creation of role-play areas in classrooms to older children's exploration of drama.
- **encouraging poetry writing**
  In *Did I Hear You Write?* Michael Rosen shows how children can be helped to reflect upon personal experiences, explore ideas and feelings, through poetry writing.

```
MY TEACHER SAYS                 ACHIEVEMENT

My teacher says I'm great at    I really wanted to swim
maths                           backwards.
and I'm sure she's right. I'm   I put the float like a pillow.
trying to do my assessment      And it worked.
test. I'm
hurricaning through the         Philip Tsohas
cards but
sometimes I hate it.

I'm not very good at reading
routes.
Sometimes I'm quite
good.
Regularly.
A piece of cake
totally.

Thomas Burton
```

Figure 8 *Poems by children which focus on 'Achievement'.*

- **helping children to reflect on investigative work**
  Children can be encouraged to stop and consider their progress during an investigation, and be given specific time on completion of the work to pause and review it.
- **recording group presentations on audio or videotape**
  Facilities to record in this way are not available in all classrooms. However, when recordings of presentations can be done, they give children an excellent opportunity to reflect on the quality of their presentation and their interaction with peers. These recordings can also be part of on-going evaluation while the presentation is in preparation.
- **sharing with children the feelings you have about your own experiences and achievements**
  Many teachers now write *with* children, recording their own experiences in diaries and stories alongside children as they work.
- **using a variety of media for self-assessment**
  Because children respond to different kinds of stimuli and work effectively in a variety of ways, it is necessary to provide them with a range of avenues for self-assessment. They may make written assessments, or find it helpful to develop their ideas on a word processor. They may enjoy opportunities for talking over assessments with you or with a friend. Some children need privacy in which to begin talking about themselves and their ideas. One child revealed his ability for self-assessment only when allowed to speak directly into a tape recorder in the privacy of the classroom stock cupboard!

The ability to reflect upon and evaluate their work is an important aspect of children's personal development and of record keeping.

It is also a significant feature of higher levels of attainment across the National Curriculum:

Mathematics AT1, Level 5
'Selecting the materials and the mathematics to use for a task, checking there is sufficient information; working methodically and reviewing progress.'

Physical Education, Level 5
'Apply aesthetic and functional criteria to their own and others' performance, and suggest how the performance could be improved.'

Art AT2, End of Key Stage Statements, Key Stage 2
'Modify their work in the light of their intentions, *the choices involved in the making process and the results.'*

Music AT1, Level 6
'Plan and present performances, and evaluate their effectiveness.'

```
I think my maths has improved a lot.
I like drawing and my favourite author
is Roald Dahl.  I enjoy football and
games and I like writing.  I wrote a good
story called 'The Day I Shrank'.


I think I have improved in reading and
a little bit in spellings.  I still like
stories.  But I've got better in tennis
and some other sports.  But I don't think
I am very good at handwriting.  I liked it
when our class went to the Tower of London
because it was interesting.


My favourite school hobby is free
writing because I can do a story of
what I like.  I like reading books.
My favourite book is Carbonel.  Mrs.
Stone says I have improved with my
reading and I think I read good too.


I think I've improved my handwriting
and I think I can improve my maths
and stories.  I don't like doing stories
much, I like doing poems better.  I don't
like some mental maths.  My new author is
Jill Murphy - The Worst Witch Stories.
```

Figure 9 *This is the first attempt by some Year 3 children to reflect upon themselves as learners.*

As children grow in confidence they can be encouraged to become more analytical of their work across the curriculum. Reviews provide opportunities for you and the children to look in greater detail at their achievements. This helps develop the quality of their self-assessments. Group work provides a further basis for analytical discussion and the quality of such work is enhanced where children are expected to record, discuss and evaluate progress together.

Older children can record their self-assessments in a number of ways. They may keep weekly log books or work planners, which allow them to track the progress of their work. Diaries can combine this kind of information with more affective responses. Selected work can be annotated by children as part of their self-assessments. In some schools this is done on special pro-formas designed for inclusion in the child's profile folder.

$\frac{3}{3}$	$\frac{10}{3}$	$\frac{24}{3}$	$\frac{28}{4}$	$\frac{5}{5}$	
$\frac{1}{2}\checkmark$	$\checkmark$	$\checkmark$	$\checkmark$	$\checkmark$	

Figure 10 *The example shows how a child assessed his own performance in PE. Each week he awarded himself marks for his cartwheel, and both the date and his assessment were recorded below his vivid illustration.*

It is important to offer children a variety of interesting ways to assess their own work, at sensible intervals, so that self-assessment does not become a boring routine. Figures 10, 11 and 12 illustrate some of the different approaches which can be tried. Teachers who have been developing self-assessment with children stress that it is necessary to be selective and not to ask children to do too much too often.

Subject	Comments	Mark
	School Report Peckham Park School Name Julia Lee July 1991	
Maths	I enjoy maths because its fun subject. I think its easy some of the sums.	A
Story	I am not quite good at story writing. Because I dont write much stories.	B
Reading	I enjoy reading because I like reading it when I read speech.	A
Science	I like Science because it is very important.	B
Art x Craft	I really enjoy Art because I am a good drawer.	A
Sport	I like Sport but I dont think it is easy because I dont do much sport	B
RE x Music	I like listening to music but I dont play any musical instruments.	B
Projects	I enjoy projects all sorts. because it is fun.	A
Spelling	I like Spelling and sometimes I get full marks and pass.	A
General Behaviour	I am very brave and a very good worker in the class	A

Figure 11 *This Year 6 child made brief comments and awarded herself grades in each area of the curriculum.*

Self Assessment

think I am good at reading, and once I start reading a good book I really get involved in it and want to get it finished. My favourite author is Enid Blyton. I don't really like the thought of writing stories, but once I start, I usually do them well. My handwriting is slanted when I write joined up but it's not too bad. I really think I am a very good drawer, even though I do not do all that much craft I love doing it. I also like doing science and doing experiments especially on electricity. On Maths I think I am good at the 4 rules, but I am a bit weak on division. As for tables I think I am good at them. I have got a computer and I write stories on it and play games on it. My favourite at the moment is Bubble Bobble. I like doing P.E, games but I am a bit less keen on dance and drama. One of the reasons I like doing games is that it involves sports and I love sports, especially football and hockey, I like climbing trees and doing rough sort of sports. My hobbies involve bike riding, reading stories by Enid Blyton, and playing on my computer. I like doing Topics made up of my own subject. eg: Nature and History.

BY OMAR

Figure 12 *Another Year 6 child used a narrative form for self-assessment.*

Management issues

Although the process of self-assessment is conducted by the child, teachers have an important management role in terms of planning and facilitating it.

You can:

- include specific activities to support self-esteem and self-assessment;
- build in time for reflection by children: examples include a brief period to review work at the end of an activity or an afternoon each term devoted to self-assessment;
- provide opportunities for children to record their own assessments;
- provide appropriate resources: for example, writing materials, notebooks, tape recorders.

Promoting self-assessment touches upon many aspects of classroom life and work across the curriculum. These need to be considered as part of a whole-school policy on assessment and record keeping, and this is considered in more detail in the section on whole-school policy (Chapters 8 and 9).

5
Using portfolios

The portfolio is a personal folder kept by each child. It contains a wide variety of evidence of achievement from within and beyond the curriculum. Out-of-school achievements can also be included in the portfolio.

Figure 13 *A child's portfolio.*

Collecting evidence of achievement for the portfolio

A young child's portfolio includes a comprehensive collection of class work, and, with guidance and encouragement from the teacher, gradually comes to incorporate some of the following forms of evidence:

- **day-to-day work**
  This may include completed writing, drawings, video and tape recordings, diagrams and maps. Sometimes it may be

more appropriate to include photographs of models or displays which children have prepared.

A child's involvement in drama, presentations, demonstrations or visits can also be illustrated effectively by photographs.

Children's workbooks, diaries and notes, together with photocopies of particular items, can also be kept in the portfolio.

- **special awards or commendations for school activities**
  Some schools have their own systems of awards in the form of certificates or cards congratulating children on an achievement. These usually cover a wide variety of extra-curricular activities and evidence of personal and social development.

- **work and awards from community schools and groups including work in languages other than English**
  Encouraging children to bring such work and awards to school strengthens community links, encourages parental involvement, provides the broadest picture of the child's development and recognises the importance of the bilingual child's first language.

- **evidence of interests and activities outside school**
  This might include photographs, drawings or writing about personal collections of stickers or stamps, membership of clubs, and activities in areas like music, sports or fund-raising. Where it is appropriate, materials, awards and certificates can be photocopied and retained in the portfolio. This may provide new aspects of achievement, upon which schools can build.

Parents need to be fully aware of the existence and purpose of the portfolio, so that they can be invited to support children in bringing evidence of interests and activities to school.

The child takes responsibility for the general management of the portfolio, including collecting the evidence and samples that make up the contents.

Selecting evidence from the portfolio for the teacher's profile folder

The review process, which is discussed fully in Chapter 3, includes an opportunity for you to look through the portfolio from time to time with the child and together select new pieces of work. This selection is then transferred to your profile folder on the child, supporting your own records of the child's development. Many of the new pieces selected may extend the record of the child's achievements, and you may feel that it is no longer necessary to retain some previously selected items in the profile folder. These items can be returned to the child.

Children's own assessments and personal criteria for selecting work are important factors in making decisions about what is retained in the profile folder. Even the youngest

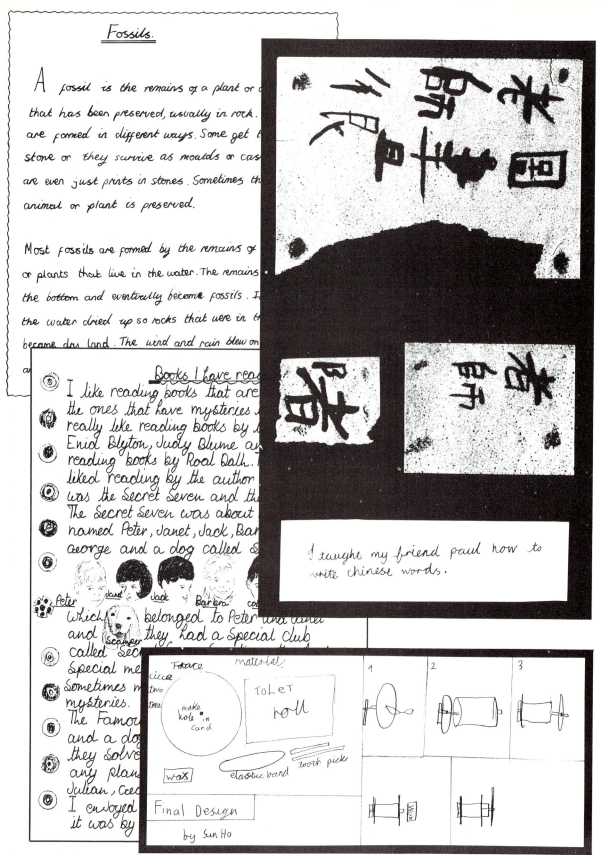

Figure 14 *Some typical examples from portfolios.*

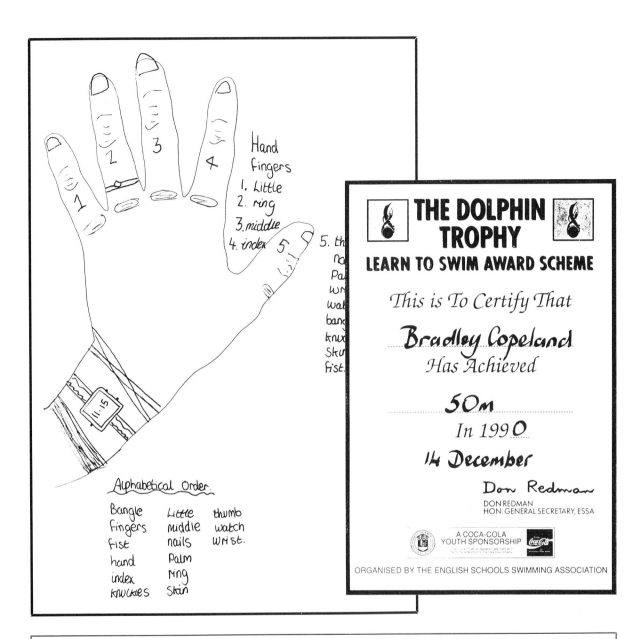

Hand

fingers
1. Little
2. ring
3. middle
4. index

5. th
na
Pa
wr
wa
band
knu
sku
Fist.

Alphabetical Order.

Bangle	Little	thumb
Fingers	Middle	watch
Fist	nails	Wrist.
hand	Palm	
index	ring	
knuckles	skin	

making an elastic band roller

what we had to do

first I drew a preliminary sketch of 3 different possible designs. I chose one design and drew a final Design then I got the materials to make the roller

Testing

Test 1 when my roller was make I tested it

number of winds (cm)	5	10	15	20	25	30
Distance travelled	19	120	139	309	441	638

Test 2 climbing slope
to make the slope I put pieces of wood under the desk leg. my roller climbed a slope of 7 cms.

children can be drawn into the selection process so that they
see that their opinions are valued and acted upon. You may
find it useful to note whether a piece of work was chosen by
yourself or the child, and the reasons established for the choice.
This information can be used in later reviews when comparison
is made with new achievements.

| SAMPLES OF WORK | Peckham Park School. |

Subject: Science   Name: Julia   Form: 4B

Earth in Space

Tides

Twice a day in most places, the waters of the Oceans rise
and fall. This rise and fall is called the TIDE. Tides are
formed mainly by the pull of the moon's gravity pulls on the
water nearest it forming twin bulges like those in the picture.
There are usually two high tides and two low tides in every
twenty-four hours. Each high tide occurs 12 hours 25 minutes after
the previous one. The Suns gravity also pulls on the Oceans but the
Sun is so far away from the Earth that its pull is not that great
as that of the moon.

WHY I CHOSE THIS SAMPLE

I chose this Science because it is a good part of
the science. I now know why we have tides and what
causes tides.

Signed: J. Lee   Date: 5th March

Figure 15 *Some schools have produced special 'sample sheets'.
Children select achievements, record them on these sheets
and add the reasons for their choice.*

Criteria for selecting evidence of achievement are very broad, yet there is a limit to the number of samples which you can retain in the profile folder. The final choice will vary, having regard both to the child's views and to what you judge to be of particular importance for any individual. Criteria for the selection may include:

- the child's own favourite pieces of work;
- work initiated by the child;
- a child's self-assessment and forward planning;
- a sample showing what you have identified as a significant point of development;
- something produced in response to a specific given task, perhaps intended for assessment purposes – you may want to note whether the child was told that this piece was in any way special, *'Do your best work . . .'* or *'I want you to take care with . . .'*, as it can be useful to compare this with the results of more open tasks or activities initiated by the child;
- work selected on pre-specified grounds – for example, you may set out to identify and collect evidence of particular achievement;
- something achieved in a context which proved especially supportive for the child;
- appropriate items from home, supplied by a parent or child, which show different aspects of development – for example, work from community schools, tape recordings of musical achievements, photocopies of certificates;
- important topic work – examples may include journals of school journeys, photographs and diaries;
- samples showing development – in particular, achievements from the beginning and end of the year illustrate development over a period of time;
- achievements in a group context;
- work showing evidence of achievement in the National Curriculum attainment targets;
- work showing a breadth of achievement beyond the National Curriculum – for example, translation work and awards for personal qualities such as persistence.

The contents of the profile folder are part of the official school record for the child and are kept by teachers. You may need to photocopy some items from the portfolio, particularly any original documents brought from home, and include the copy in the profile folder. It is important that the agreement of parents and children is obtained before material from home is photocopied.

The profile folder continues to develop during the year, as some samples are removed or replaced, and others inserted. The audience for its contents includes the parents and other teachers.

Selecting these samples for the teacher's profile folder is an important part of the review and forward planning process. It also provides you with a valuable source of evidence and supports the child's personal development by:

- fostering a sense of control over her or his own learning by encouraging reviews of work, recognition of achievement and the making of personal choices;
- encouraging the child's sense of pride in her or his work and thereby building self-esteem;
- reflecting the all-round development of the child, both within and beyond the National Curriculum foundation subjects;
- promoting parental involvement;
- providing information for a receiving teacher;
- providing evidence of achievement for moderation at the end of Key Stages.

In selecting samples throughout the year for the profile folder, it is necessary to keep in mind what is needed at the end of the year for inclusion in the annual summary records and the fuller records for use by children when they move between primary schools or transfer to secondary schools (see Chapter 7).

Annual summary records

At the end of each year, in a summative review, items are selected from the portfolio and profile folder for inclusion in the teacher's annual summary record for the child, which goes forward to the next class. Any remaining evidence of achievement belonging to the child is returned. If teachers wish, each child may have an opportunity to make a scrapbook or folder that gives a personal record of achievement for the year.

In years when children transfer between schools (most usually in Year 6) a more detailed record of achievement can be produced by children. This entails a very careful selection of evidence of achievement and a personal statement by the child, and is discussed more fully in Chapter 7.

Management issues

As each portfolio belongs to the child, you can encourage all children to contribute to classroom management by taking charge of their own portfolio and accepting the responsibility for collecting and storing work and other evidence of achievement.

Children can also be encouraged to annotate items. This might begin as quite a simple record of the date the work was started and completed. When you are talking with a child during reviews, you might suggest that brief notes explaining the context of some pieces of work should be put into the portfolio. More detailed self-assessments of some pieces by older children can gradually be introduced.

All these records can be of great assistance to teachers in the management of recording and assessment, as well as informing review discussions.

Children need to be supplied with suitable folders to house the evidence making up the portfolio and give them a degree of confidentiality. Some schools prefer to keep art work separately rather than fold and damage items. Other schools photograph art and three-dimensional work, and performances and presentations by children.

The storage of portfolios is important. Easy access is needed at all times if the children are to take effective responsibility for the management of portfolios. Some ways in which teachers have provided this access include:

- using wheeled tubs, stored under tables;
- using individual trays or designated cupboard space;
- having a classroom cupboard door removed to give children quick and easy access to portfolios stored on shelves;
- using a lateral filing system for economy of space (filing cabinets are sometimes used by teachers but these are of limited value, becoming unstable if more than one drawer is opened).

Good storage arrangements not only help classroom organisation but also ensure that the portfolios are valued and given status.

SECTION THREE

Summary Records

This section shows how schools can use records of achievement to meet the statutory requirements to report on children's progress. Information is provided on what these requirements are, and there is critical consideration of ways in which a professional report can be written. The compiling and using of summary records of achievement when the child moves class and school are also considered.

6
Reporting to parents

The legal framework for reporting

Requirements

School reports to parents now have a legal framework, and teachers have statutory duties, spelt out in regulations which are summarised as follows:

- a written report on each primary pupil's achievement must reach her or his parents by 31 July in each year. The requirement to report starts from the year in which pupils are first liable to follow the National Curriculum attainment targets and programmes of study in the subject concerned;
- all reports have to cover:
  –pupil performance in all National Curriculum subjects
  –results of public examinations
  –brief particulars of achievements in other subjects and activities undertaken during the year
  –comment on attendance;
- at the end of Key Stages only, reports must give the level of achievement, on the 1–10 scale, by Profile Component and Subject for any foundation subject where Orders apply. Schools are not required to *report* achievement by attainment target, but at the end of Key Stages parents have a right of access to records which contain this information;
- reports must make clear where pupils have been exempted from any attainment target.

Formats for reports

It is for individual schools to decide upon the exact design of their reports. The DES have provided a suggested national reporting format. Most local education authorities are also providing advice and in many cases offer their own LEA

Figure 16 *The statutory information in this LEA reporting format is well organised, with provision for an overview (Approaches to Learning) plus subject specific comment. Space has been provided for a range of additional information, such as details of a child's languages, child and parent comment, and learning targets (Plans and Priorities). (Reproduced by kind permission of the London Borough of Hammersmith and Fulham.)*

reporting format for schools to consider. Some schools may prefer to use a format linked with their approach to assessment and recording, for example those schools using the *Primary Learning Record*.

The reporting framework is particularly important when children are moving between primary and secondary phases of education. This is dealt with in more detail in Chapter 7.

Advice for parents from the DES

The DES has provided parents with details of what to expect in their child's report at Key Stage 1. Schools need to have in mind what parents have been told:

What's in the report?

Whatever school your child is at, you might expect the report to show:

■ the results for your child in English, maths and science based on the national tests of last term and their classroom work over the past couple of years;

■ the teacher's explanation of what the achievements mean;

■ a report by the teacher on your child's progress in other subjects;

■ a note of his or her attendance; and

■ a note of his or her achievements in other activities.

Overall, the report will tell you what your child has learned, and what he or she is good at or may need extra help with. It should also give you some practical ideas about what you, the parent, can do to help your child in the future.

Figure 17 (*From* Your Child's Report – What it means and how it can help, *DES, May 1991. Reproduced with the permission of the Controller of Her Majesty's Stationery Office.*)

Additionally, the DES suggest that parents should know the 'informal status' of National Curriculum assessments if schools decide to give an idea of levels in National Curriculum subjects in years other than at the end of a Key Stage. Parents should be told:

'The National Curriculum levels shown in this report have not been formally tested in the way they will be [next year], but are based on your child's work over the past year.'

(*Reporting To Parents: Some suggestions for primary teachers*, DES, 1991.)

Providing a reference for assessments

The audience for the report is the parents, the child and the receiving teacher and school. It should present them with relevant information on the child's development to date and provide a constructive basis from which they can help the child to move forward in the following year. The three main references for a teacher's judgements are discussed below.

Criterion-referencing

This describes assessment *'on the basis of the quality of the performance of a pupil irrespective of the performance of other pupils'* (Report by the Task Group on Assessment and Testing, 1987).

Clear statements of what a child can do in any area can be described as criterion-referenced. In particular, teacher comment is criterion-referenced when an individual child's performance is being discussed in terms of the National Curriculum attainment targets.

Norm-referencing

This is the system which has been used for many public examinations where *'pupils are placed in rank order and pre-determined proportions are placed in the various grades'* (Report by the Task Group on Assessment and Testing, 1987).

In terms of the primary classroom, teachers use norm-referencing more loosely, to place children's performance in relation to other children in the class. It is well understood by parents, who like to know how their children's work compares with that of their peers.

In the context of a record of achievement, however, norm-referencing needs to be handled with care. The creation of 'league tables' of performance within a classroom can rapidly destroy children's self-esteem which a teacher has worked hard to build up.

Self-referencing (ipsative-referencing)

Self-referencing is concerned with the progress of individual children over a period of time, comparing present achievement with previous achievement. It is particularly valuable in making the kind of formative assessment which feeds into target setting and planning of work for individuals.

Self-referencing illustrates the 'value added' by the work of a teacher with a child, and is an important additional consideration in any published information on the performance of pupils against National Curriculum criteria.

Developing the quality of reports

The need for clear referencing

Children's progress can therefore be assessed against

- specific criteria
- the performance of others in the class
- or their own previous performance.

Each form of referencing may be used in reporting. However, reports become muddled and ambiguous when the reference for assessment is unclear and when information is poorly organised.

In *Reporting To Parents*, the DES make suggestions for an 'overview at the beginning of a report'. This 'overview' shows, quite unintentionally, how confusing a poorly organised and carelessly referenced summary can become:

SOCIAL AND EMOTIONAL DEVELOPMENT

An overview at the beginning of the report is a good way to bring in the wider matters that the parent will also want to know about:

Joy tries hard and is showing increasing confidence in all areas of the curriculum. Progress is slow, and she often has to struggle to keep up. She has great difficulty in her number work but her reading has really improved. Her work in technology compares well with others in the class. Joy's behaviour is more mature and she now joins in happily with all classroom activities. She has one special friend and gets on well with other children.

Figure 18 (*From* Reporting To Parents: Some suggestions for primary teachers, *DES, 1991. Reproduced with the permission of the Controller of Her Majesty's Stationery Office.*)

The reader is left with a confused impression of a child who has had a range of personal, social and cognitive difficulties, the present levels of which are somehow elusive. General comments such as *'Progress is slow'* and *'she often has to struggle to keep up'*, sit uneasily alongside statements that *'reading has really improved'* and *'technology compares well'*. No reasons, evidence or examples are given, and analysis shows that a major cause of confusion is the reference for these comments, which can only be guessed at in many cases.

The inconsistencies in referencing are indicated below:

Comment	Reference
'Joy tries hard and is showing increasing confidence in all areas of the curriculum.'	Self-referencing.
'Progress is slow . . .'	What is the reference? Is this progress slow against National Curriculum criteria, in comparison with others in the class or with her own previous progress?
'. . . and she often has to struggle to keep up.'	What is the reference? Is she struggling in comparison with her peers?
'She has great difficulty in her number work . . .'	What is the reference?
'. . . but her reading has really improved.'	What is the reference?
'Her work in technology compares well with others in the class.'	Clear norm-referencing, but contradicts earlier generalised statement of difficulties.
'Joy's behaviour is more mature and she now joins in happily with all classroom activities.'	Self-referencing or norm-referencing?
'She has one special friend and gets on well with other children.'	Criterion-referencing.

The problem is compounded because these loose, frequently unreferenced and contradictory comments jumble together remarks about the child's personal and social development with what are no more than fragments of information on her cognitive development and academic performance. There is no consistency in comments relating to the curriculum; technology is mentioned, science is not. Mathematics is referred to purely in terms of number work and English in terms of reading. More thought should have been given to the structure of the report and the organisation of information.

Organising a professional report

A professionally written report should give a reasoned analysis of a child's achievement, highlight the further needs of the child and indicate how these might be met. All this information needs to be organised in ways which will give readers:

- a broad picture of the child, through an overview;
- information in more depth on individual aspects of the child's development.

The extensive information and evidence gathered in a record of achievement will support report writing in all these areas.

An overview
In an overview there can be discussion on the development of the child's personal qualities and social skills within the context of the school. This would detail individual strengths and areas of development since the last report (self-referencing) and mention, where appropriate, any marked difference with the development of her or his peers to which parents' attention should be drawn (norm-referencing).

Teachers' observations of a child's interaction with peers will be the basis for this comment, supplemented by records from reviews which consider a child's achievement in the light of her or his own perceptions.

A report on personal and social development should respect the child, avoiding any generalised and unsubstantiated comment, whether complimentary or not, for example:

> *'a sweet little girl'*   *'a lazy child'*
> *'talks too much'*   *'could do better'*

Curriculum progress should be discussed only in general terms in an overview. In Joy's case the report might need to convey a high degree of effort in all areas but more progress in some than in others.

Subject-specific comment on the foundation subjects
This can be more detailed and analytical. Information should

be given on a child's achievement and interest in the subject, perhaps noting contexts which have proved particularly supportive. Clear use of appropriate references for assessment can be made by considering:

- What are the child's achievements in relation to stated criteria?
- How much progress has the child made since the last report?
- Are there significant issues which necessitate comparison with the general achievement within the class?

Parents need a statement of what the child knows, understands and can do with reference to the National Curriculum attainment targets. At the end of Key Stages, this part of the report needs to provide levels of attainment for Profile Components and Subjects. Work samples retained in the teacher's profile folder provide a basis for this comment and offer supporting evidence.

This part of the report should also describe the child's needs within a specific area and any action taken to meet those needs. Where new targets have been agreed upon for the coming year, these can be recorded. Evidence is supplied by records of reviews with the child.

Achievement in areas beyond the National Curriculum

A statement of the child's achievements in other areas and a note of any special gifts, talents or interests can be provided. The broad evidence of achievement gathered from within and outside school will support this.

Comment by the child

An opportunity can be provided for the child to comment on the report. The ability of children to contribute to a report, and the quality of their comment, draws on skills developed through self-assessment.

Response by the parent

Provision can be made for parents to comment. This is particularly appropriate where parents have been kept informed and involved in recognising and recording achievement.

Commenting on weaknesses

Although the focus of a record of achievement is on *achievement in all areas*, the needs of the child for further help are fully recognised in the review process and acted upon through the setting of agreed targets.

Reports based on this information can clarify areas where a child has had difficulty and suggest ways forward.

This kind of constructive professional comment can be particularly helpful for the long-term development of the child, whereas the kinds of general criticism recommended by the DES are likely to be less helpful.

To illustrate this point, the following example is from the guidance for parents in *Your Child's Report*:

> *"Mary enjoys reading... but she makes mistakes when she reads aloud."*
>
> Although Mary was at level 2 in 'Reading', the report advised her parents that she could do even better with help.
>
> *"Any encouragement you can give her at home to read with you, and to sit and read to herself, would be useful."*

Figure 19 *(From* 'Your Child's Report – What it means and how it can help'*, DES, May 1991. Reproduced with the permission of the Controller of Her Majesty's Stationery Office.)*

These remarks could have been written after the most cursory observation by any intelligent adult. They put the child in error, and offer no explanation or advice beyond what amounts to 'more practice'. Yet apparently the level of the problem is such that it needs to be mentioned in an annual report.

Professional comment should indicate why a child is having problems; where advice is offered to parents it should be reasoned and precise.

Using the example above, comment should provide answers to questions such as:

- Does Mary have difficulty with some or all texts?
- What kinds of text has she been encouraged to read aloud?
- Does she have difficulty with specific texts, or is she a competent reader who has difficulty reading all texts aloud, even simple texts that she can read for herself and talk about?

The DES example does not differentiate between even these most basic possibilities. Yet most children, and adults too, make mistakes in reading aloud texts they find difficult.

Supposing the latter possibility to be the case, the teacher may have observed that Mary lacks confidence and would have talked this over with her in a review session. The teacher's professional advice would reflect this.

For example, after commenting on Mary's development since the last report, the teacher would set out her achievements and her needs. Part of her report might read something like this:

'Mary can read a supportive text independently, and is able to discuss the plot and give reasons for her views. She has a wide taste in books, both fiction and non-fiction, and enjoys reading, often choosing to read quietly to herself.

However, when reading aloud Mary makes many mistakes, even with simple texts that she knows well. She appears anxious when reading aloud and seldom chooses to do so, even from her favourite books. When we reviewed her achievements, Mary explained that she finds it difficult to read aloud because she is afraid of making mistakes. We have planned ways to develop her confidence, and agreed targets for the coming year.'

Involving parents

The DES documents encourage the active involvement of parents in supporting their children. In *Reporting to Parents* they acknowledge that *'A careful judgement has to be made as to what it might be realistic to ask them to do'*, but effective advice for parents needs to reflect the professionalism of the teacher and must therefore go beyond the bland suggestion that a child like Mary needs more practice.

Advice needs to address such questions as:

- What kinds of material should she be encouraged to read aloud at home, at what level of difficulty and for what audience?
- What should parents do when Mary makes a mistake: ignore it, note it, stop and correct her or ask her to read again?

For support to be effective, it is important that parents are able to make the most appropriate response, and the teacher needs to give advice based upon her or his diagnosis of Mary's problem.

Parents may need advice on how to work with the child. For example, material for reading aloud should always be prepared by the child and the National Curriculum statements acknowledge this in references to reading aloud 'familiar texts'. However, parents may not realise this and might be advised to allow children to read something quietly to themselves before reading it aloud.

The context for reading aloud at home may need to be the focus for advice. Perhaps Mary should be encouraged to read simple stories, or short poems that she knows and enjoys, to a younger sibling. Perhaps she should take home copies of a two- or three-character play so that the family could join in with the reading and have some fun. A teacher's professional advice to parents would stress the need for Mary's reading aloud to have purpose and enjoyment and not merely to be an agonising daily drill, if her skills are to develop well.

Advice in a report needs to be expressed concisely and to concentrate on the most important needs of any individual child, but, clearly, it must also reflect the expertise of the teacher.

Management issues

The problem for teachers is that many reports need to be written within a short period during a particularly busy time at the end of the year, when teachers are at their most tired and stressed. After writing the first few reports it can gradually become more and more difficult to find words which are fresh and sharp enough to describe accurately individual experiences. Reports can easily come to resemble a self-assembly package of standard comments. Some schools have used 'statement banks' in an attempt both to support the teacher and to make the standard comments more worthwhile, but the use of statement banks often results in reports which lack individuality and relevance.

However, there are other supportive measures which are worth consideration:

- **the comprehensive collection of evidence, contextual notes, teacher observations and accounts of reviews within the pupil profile provides superb material for an individual report**
  The final summative review between child and teacher allows this evidence to be drawn together as a basis for highly relevant comment across each area. If these summative reviews with children can be organised over a number of weeks and individual reports are written immediately afterwards, this gives individual report writing a particular focus and also helps to spread the workload.
- **word processors offer further opportunities for reducing the burden of report writing**
  As they gradually become more available and familiar, teachers can use them throughout the year to draft notes on each child's progress. These notes can be updated as appropriate. A final redraft can be undertaken in the Summer term and with the use of a printer, reports can be given high quality presentation.

Good management of report writing therefore involves a programme of work which is spread out over the year, then drawn together and focused during the summer term. Careful planning is important, particularly in years when children transfer between schools, and a suggested timetable for planning work over the whole year is provided in Chapter 7.

7
Supporting children when they change classes and schools

The processes underlying records of achievement enable children's development to be mapped and supported throughout their school life. The quality of information provided by these records, and the children's involvement in creating them, mean that records of achievement also play a central role in ensuring children a smooth transition between schools.

Family circumstances may necessitate a change of school for children at any time. Where children have collected a portfolio of work they can be encouraged to take this with them to their new school. The necessary documents from the teacher's profile folder, with selected samples, can pass directly from school to school and provide the receiving teacher with comprehensive information and evidence of achievement.

Most children change class at the end of a year within their own school, but there are particularly significant years in which children change schools. For many children the most important change is at the end of Year 6, at transfer from primary to secondary education.

Compiling records of achievement when children change classes

Towards the end of each year it is important to hold a summative review with the child, focusing on the year's achievements. The final selection of work samples can be made for inclusion in the annual summary folder which is passed on to the next teacher. The child's own assessments, written by the child or recorded by the teacher, can be included, together with targets for the coming year and an appropriate selection of teacher records. A copy of the child's final report can be added when this is ready and – at the end of Key Stages – an assessment of the child's level of achievement in the foundation subjects.

You might also wish to encourage your children to make their own annual records of achievement. These can include samples of work from their portfolios and other evidence of achievement. Annual records of achievement can take any form which you feel is appropriate for particular children or year groups; some teachers encourage children to make personal achievement scrapbooks or create their own folders to take samples of work.

Compiling records of achievement when children change schools

At the time of transfer, a number of special issues need to be considered relating to records of achievement.

These issues concern:

- the statutory framework relating to the transfer of records;
- the rights of parents to reports and access to records;
- the personal needs of children and their parents;
- the needs of schools.

The statutory framework relating to the transfer of records

Regulations on School Records 1989 and the accompanying DES Circular set out the requirements for the transfer of school records. From September 1989, these regulations require primary schools to provide, on request, their records on a child to any receiving school.

The regulations also require, from 1 September 1990, the disclosure of the pupil's record, upon request, to any school considering the pupil for admission. There are a number of categories of records which are exempt from disclosure, including those made before 1 September 1990.

The rights of parents to reports and access to records

- **Reports**
  Schools are required by the regulations to provide a written report to parents annually, as detailed in Chapter 6. When children are changing schools, particularly at the end of Key Stages, a clear summary of their children's strengths and improvements is important. It is also a valuable opportunity to set out the areas in which children need to develop or where particular support might be necessary.
- **Access to school records**
  Schools are also required by the regulations governing school records to allow parents access to school's educational records at any time within their child's education if they give 15 days' written notice. The involvement of parents in their children's records of achievement can be an important way of providing access when children are changing schools.

The personal needs of children

Reaching the end of their final year in primary school is an important stage for all children. They are aware of the transition through childhood represented by their moving into secondary school. Recognition of their achievement at this time is important.

The needs of schools

- **The needs of primary schools**
  Primary teachers need assurance that the schools to which their children transfer are making use of the primary records of achievement.
- **The needs of secondary schools**
  Secondary schools need clear summaries of children's achievement which they can use: for the purposes of induction, curriculum planning, grouping, identification of special educational needs.

The content of records of achievement when children change schools

The issues raised above can be addressed by providing:

- a personal record of achievement, written and owned by each child, which can be produced in a special folder and presented at the end of the summer term;
- a teacher's record of achievement for each child which is sent on to the receiving school.

Children's personal records of achievement

Children's personal records of achievement are an effective way to mark this stage, particularly if the children are clear about their ownership of the record and the ways they can use it to help introduce themselves at their next school.

These personal records of achievement are separate from the official records passed between teachers. They are created by children themselves during the course of their final year, and can include:

- the personal statement, sometimes made into a book;
- a selection of work samples showing achievement;
- a copy of the final school report.

Many children now contribute their own self-assessments to records and reports, and some schools have extended this so that in the final primary year it becomes a full review of achievement produced by the children for inclusion in their personal record of achievement.

The child's personal statement

In the personal statement, children can be encouraged to review and write about their achievements, interests and activities both within and beyond school. Areas you may wish children to cover in their statements are shown in Figure 20.

SUGGESTED ELEMENTS

I   Me: – Description of myself as introduction eg – name, age, physique, etc. (This section could concentrate on introducing the pupil)

II   Me at Home

Where I live
Friends and family
What I like doing (hobbies, clubs, sport, pets, etc.)

III   Me at School

What I enjoy doing at school
What I'm good at
Books I have read
Things I have made
Some interesting things I have found out about
Other activities – music music, sport, craft, using library, class activities – plays etc.
Special responsibilities – eg helping young children, library monitor etc.
School journeys and expeditions

IV   My Achievements

What I have achieved this year, both at home and at school, ie work, behaviour, helping others, things I have made, your talents, eg music, drama, drawing, model making, sewing, singing , craftwork, etc.

V   Looking forward to Secondary School

What you think it will be like, describe any visits you have made
What you are looking forward to at your new school
Have you got any friends or relations there? What do you hope to achieve when you go to secondary school?

Figure 20 *This suggested framework for personal statements was supplied by a secondary school to its partner primaries as part of primary/secondary liaison work.*

The statements can be hand-written, produced on a word processor or consist mainly of drawings and photographs, whichever seems most appropriate for the child.

This activity provides a natural focus of interest and fits well into the curriculum for the spring and summer terms of Year 6.

Most children respond well to this activity. Very few feel threatened, and these can be supported by introducing the work gradually and giving plenty of opportunities to try out ideas and see how other children are setting about their statements.

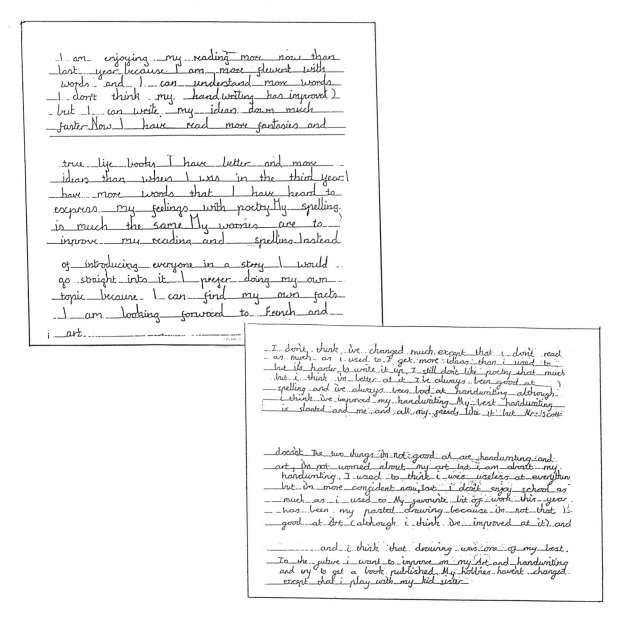

Figure 21 *Many annual reporting formats now provide for comment by children on their year's work.*

THE FUTURE

What i want to do in the future is to become a good pupil in sports and other things at Bonus Pastor Secondry school. When i leave school id like to go to college maybe even university if im clever enough. When im an adult if i find a job and a house in the Caribean ill go over to live there so that i can see my family when i want to. I'd like to get married and have kids. I'd like to carry on doing some sports as i like it and think im quite good at it too. I like to travel so when i grow id like to go to a lot of different countries. I don't know what job i want to do yet. But i might try to become a doctor or journalist or maybe even a scientist. My ambition is to invent or discover something really important.

At home I have to make my mum lots of cups of tea. I make my bed. I help tidy up my home. I wash up sometimes and help with the dinner.

I have a hobby. It is collecting football stickers. I have a book to put them in. I do it every year - all together four years. I do it in my bedroom because when I get a good one I tend to shout. I play sport from Monday to Friday. I play football in my school. We play class 2. We nearly always beat them. I don't need a special kit. I support Liverpool FC. I don't have any badges for football.

When I think of what nature I am, I am a good person. I am grumpy sometimes. If I sit with my arms crossed I am not in a good mood. I am happy if I see something funny. I don't fight a lot, only sometimes. I say I am loyal to my friends. I always stick by them.

I also do swimming. I am very good. I have got many certificates this year. I can draw but I am not good. That's why I try to draw better. I can draw spaceships very well. PE and games are brilliant. I like rounders because I can bat the ball far and low. I also very much enjoy when we do headstands and cartwheels. I can't do forward rolls.

In English we do reading and writing. Writing is my favourite thing. I like writing stories. I write some at home for my mum. I don't play any musical instruments but I would like to play the violin. I'm not so good at mathematics but I am all right. I get most of my work right. History is good because we find out about other people who lived years and years ago. I liked the Pilgrim Fathers the most because of the dangers they took. Paintings I like because I am quite good at looking at a picture. I am trying to paint. Science is very good. I like it when we made parachutes. Mine didn't drop very well but it didn't matter.

Figure 22 *These extracts are taken from personal statements written by children at transfer to secondary school. The personal statements cover many areas of children's experience, in and out of school, and set out their hopes for the future.*

All children need appropriate support in presenting themselves well. Your guidance can include:

- reading from a previous statement, with the owner's permission;
- providing a framework of 'chapter headings' which focus clearly on achievement;
- encouraging children to share their statement as it develops. Children may begin by sharing with a friend or a small group of friends, then move on to presenting work to the whole class. This activity offers you important assessment opportunities across attainment targets;
- promoting a good balance in their writing;
- intervening more directly where children have written autobiographical details of a highly personal nature. You can explain possible audiences for the personal statement and suggest the statement is written for a particular audience in mind.

A selection of work samples showing achievement

The personal statement can be accompanied by pieces of written work, video and audio tapes and certificates for activities and interests undertaken within and beyond school.

The collection of work samples is considered in detail in Chapter 5.

A copy of the final school report

Some schools may wish children to have their own copy of their final school report included in the record of achievement folder.

Reports are considered in detail in Chapter 6.

Presenting the personal record of achievement

Some schools provide a special folder for the personal record of achievement in which each child can put the statement and samples. They sometimes like to include the child's photograph on the front.

When the personal record of achievement has been compiled, many schools organise a special ceremony at which there can be a formal presentation of the folders to the children. At transition this celebrates children's achievement over a long period, and underlines the value and purpose of what they have done. Such a presentation also provides an opportunity to communicate this sense of value to younger children in the primary school as they begin to create their own records.

Children can take their personal record of achievement to interviews at secondary schools where it forms the basis of discussion. Many secondary schools have found that the record is also particularly useful during induction.

The teacher's records of achievement for each child .

At the time of transfer, secondary schools welcome children arriving with their own personal record of achievement. The secondary schools also need formal records for each child and these should be compiled from the teacher's profile folder and handed on by the primary school. At secondary school a number of teachers need access to this information, and it may be appropriate to organise some notes, work samples and other evidence from the primary teacher's profile folder in a subject-specific way. Receiving teachers also need immediate access to end-of-Key-Stage assessment results.

The teacher's record of achievement for each child should contain the following:

- a summary of attainment across the National Curriculum;

```
What you will do today
```

Period 1   *WELCOME*

Period 2   *MEETING YOUR TUTOR*

Period 3   *SCIENCE*

Break

Period 4   *P.E.*

Period 5   *ENGLISH*

Lunch

Period 6   *FRENCH*

Period 7   *MATHS*

Period 8   *PHOTOGRAPH*

HOMEWORK DIARIES

GETTING YOUR VIEWS

```
How did you get on?
```

We hope you have enjoyed today. If you have found many
things here different from your primary school, don't
be worried. You will soon get used to the school.
Try answering the questions below to let us know how you
got on:

1. Can you remember the names of any of your new
   classmates or teachers?

2. Which parts of your record of achievement did you talk
   about with your tutor?

3. What experiments did you do in Science?

4. What did you do during break?

5. What parts of the P.E. and English lessons did you
   like best?

6. Was lunch enjoyable? What did you eat?

7. Did you enjoy the activities in French and Maths?

8. How much have you written in your homework diary?

9. Which part of the day did you like best?

10. Were there any parts of the day you didn't enjoy?

11. Do you have any other comments?

PLEASE remember to give in your comments to your tutor
before you leave.

Figure 23 *A secondary induction programme for Year 6 children which makes use of their primary record of achievement.*

- a summary of the curriculum coverage;
- for bilingual children, a recognition of their first language and, as appropriate, a statement of their competence in both first language and English;
- a copy of the child's final Year 6 report;
- one or two examples of the child's work which illustrate aspects of development within the National Curriculum;
- evidence of achievement beyond the National Curriculum, for example, certificates for playing musical instruments;
- a clear statement of the child's learning needs – reference should be made to any special difficulties and details given of any specific action taken or strategies used, and their degree of success.

PRIMARY SCHOOL

Timetable for Year 6

Autumn term

- receive feedback from secondary school
- begin processes for new records of achievement
- gather evidence and information if a portfolio needs to be started
- begin art work for bookmaking, where appropriate
- keep parents informed of the processes to be undertaken during the year
- have regard for the requirements on Key Stage reporting
- carry out reviews and update the teacher's profile folder;
- talk with the children about how to prepare their records of achievement

Spring term

- arrange for children to begin their personal statement of achievement
- organise time for children to share their draft personal statement with peers
- guide children in the selection of samples from their portfolios to support their personal statement and provide a rounded picture of personal interests and achievements
- update parents
- begin summative reviews

Summer term

First half of term

- organise finalising of children's personal statements, making into a book where appropriate, and putting these with supporting documents into each child's record of achievement folder
- arrange for children to present their completed records of achievement to the class
- arrange summative reviews for teacher and child, with the children receiving feedback on presentation in preparation for secondary school interviews
- use information on the children from the teacher's profile folder, the summative review and the results of Key Stage assessments to complete final report to parents and the receiving secondary school
- arrange any visits from secondary teachers
- add copies of reports to the records to be forwarded to secondary schools

Second half of term

- arrange for children to use record of achievement at interview
- provide copy of reports for parents

SECONDARY SCHOOL

Timetable for primary links

Autumn term
- use primary records of achievement; displays, follow-up work and discussion between form tutors and pupils to assist with getting to know each other
- organise any appropriate feedback from children to primary schools, for example letters to children in Year 6
- review relevance of information provided:
    What was used effectively to benefit children?
    What additional information was needed?
- provide feedback for primary schools on transition process

Spring term
- maintain contact with primary schools
- review approaches to curriculum and monitor children's learning experiences

Summer term
First half of term
- visit primary schools
- receive records on the child from primary schools
Second half of term
- interview primary children, using records of achievement
- use records to distribute information about curriculum areas to subject staff, Year Heads and tutors for grouping purposes
- use records of achievement at induction

Figure 24 *A timetable for transfer*

Timing the transfer of teacher records is very important. Secondary schools need records as near to half term in the Summer Term as possible. If there are delays in transferring records beyond this date, it is more difficult to plan the composition of class groups and the curriculum for Year 7.

It is hoped that the Assessment Orders for Key Stage 2 will fully recognise timing factors relating to transfer.

An example of a two-year timetable bridging transfer is given at the end of this chapter in Figure 24.

Management issues

Many of the management issues related to the processes of recording achievement during the final year of primary school are similar to those in other years. These issues are dealt with in other chapters of this handbook.

Timing is the most important management issue specific to transfer and a suggested timetable for primary classes is set out in Figure 24. This chart also suggests a timetable for secondary school staff organising primary links.

As mentioned earlier in this chapter, children, parents, primary teachers and receiving secondary teachers all have clear needs at this time of transfer. It is important that school policy fully recognises and meets these needs, helping children to view transfer as an exciting and stimulating time for them. School policy needs to take account of the two records of achievement discussed in this chapter:

- the child's personal record of achievement, created and owned by the child;
- the formal teacher records of achievement for each child which belong to the primary school and are passed directly to the secondary school.

Many Local Education Authorities provide useful support to schools in relation to the transfer of children from primary to secondary school. This support involves:

- providing advice on a common approach to summarising achievement at the end of Year 6;
- giving guidelines on the timing for transfer of records and secondary school interviews.

SECTION FOUR

Whole-school Policy

This section provides some practical advice on the variety of recording formats which teachers may wish to consider. It also describes the ways in which teachers can work together to develop a coherent whole-school approach to recording and reporting through records of achievement.

8
Planning and recording

Providing a framework

The processes involved in creating records of achievement together with the contents of the records, provide important opportunities to integrate planning, record-keeping and assessment.

- **Samples of work** collected in children's portfolios provide a wide range of recorded evidence reflecting all aspects of development on which you can draw.
- **Children's self-assessments,** together with comments added by parents, are a good way of encouraging involvement and giving a broader perspective on personal and social development.
- **Reviews of children's achievement** allow all this information to be used formatively as you identify areas of progress and need with the individuals concerned, agree targets and plan together how these can be met. Reviews can serve as the basis for the important aspects of differentiation within curriculum planning as a whole.

Figure 25 shows one way in which recording achievement can support curriculum planning and assessment.

This chart is very detailed, and it is not intended that every curriculum area should be mapped in this way. This example is included to show the relevance of record of achievement processes to the vital areas of formative assessment, recording and planning.

Keeping a variety of records

Schools are using a variety of formats for the recording of achievement, and of attainment within the National Curriculum. As already noted, such records can be integrated with a record of achievement approach. For example, the Primary Language and Learning Records, which are being

Curriculum planning areas		What will be assessed	How assessment can be recorded
Reading aloud with teacher Talking with teacher	Interest in reading NC En2	Understanding NC En2 Independence NC En2 Skills NC En2 Response to text NC En1 Response to text NC En2	**Recording by teacher:** informal notes, running records and miscue (see PLR Handbook for descriptive details) (Profile) **Recording by ancillary staff:** notes on what was read, difficulties and level of interest (Profile)
Quiet reading		Ability to read silently NC En2 Independence NC En2 Concentration NC En2 Persistence NC En2	**Recording by teacher:** written observations (Profile) **Self-assessment by child:** descriptive comment, written or tape recorded; book reviews; completed proforma (Portfolio)
Group reading aloud with peers		Independence NC En2 Understanding NC En2 Confidence NC En2	**Recording by teacher:** written observations; tape recordings (Profile)
Reading at home (for example, PACT)		Independence NC En2 Understanding NC En2 Responding to text NC En1 Responding to text NC En2	**Recording by parent:** enjoyment, what was read and any difficulties (Portfolio)
Skills work		Grapho-phonic skills NC En2 Grapho-phonic skills NC En4 Word recognition skills NC En2	**Products:** work sheets (Portfolio) **Recording by teacher:** written observations; notes of questions (Profile) **Recording by ancillary staff:** behaviour; child's need for support (Profile)
Listening to stories, information books read aloud		Response to text NC En1 Response to text NC En2 Understanding NC En2 Listening skills NC En1 Questioning NC En1	**Recording by teacher:** written observations; adequacy of book provision (Profile) **Recording by ancillary staff:** what was read; level of interest, child's comment (Profile)
Written book reviews		Understanding NC En2 Response to text NC En2 Silent reading NC En2 Independence NC En2 Writing NC En3	**Products:** written evidence with annotation by child or teacher (Portfolio)
Links with topic work		Information retrieval skills NC En2 Writing NC En3 Writing NC En4 Writing NC En5	**Products:** written evidence with annotation by child or teacher (Portfolio)
Presentations to group, class and school		Response to text NC En1 Response to text NC En2 Understanding NC En2 Presentations & collaborative work NC En1	**Recording by teacher:** written observations (Profile) **Products:** photographs, audio and video tape recordings with annotations by child or teacher (Portfolio)

Formative uses of recorded assessment	Issues relating to curriculum planning
Reviews	**Evaluation of planning for the class**
Termly or half-termly	Adequacy of resources provided
Review of all work and notes in portfolio and profile by teacher and child	Adequacy of time provided
Recognition of achievement	Effectiveness of record keeping
Updating of profile to reflect achievement	**Revised planning for the child**
Consideration of how child sees her or himself as a reader	What further resources should be offered?
Consideration of how child perceives her or his own skills in self-assessment	What skills development needs to be supported?
	What groupings could be tried?
Establishmnent of targets and support to be given	Would paired work be useful?
Self-assessment	What advice needs to be given to parents?
Termly timetabled session for child to review and update the quality of self-assessment	What further stimulus is needed?
Opportunity to talk with teacher	What extra help is needed?

Figure 25 *Integrating curriculum planning, assessment and recording through records of achievement.*

This detailed breakdown has been provided as an example to demonstrate the supportive aspects of records of achievement. It is not intended as a blueprint for curriculum planning.

introduced widely in schools, share important principles and practices with records of achievement, such as:

- focusing on recording achievement;
- recognising all aspects of children's development;
- involving children through conferences/reviews;
- providing opportunities for children to contribute to their own records;
- collecting and retaining samples of work;
- involving parents.

Whatever a school's recording system, it needs to be sufficiently flexible to be able to accommodate different recording needs. A coherent whole-school approach is necessary; coherence does not necessarily mean, however, that one approach to recording in all areas of the curriculum needs to be adopted. There are valid reasons why records should be different in certain areas. The important thing is that school policy has identified common requirements which incorporate different approaches.

Whole-school approach

A whole-school approach enables records to be interpreted relatively simply and quickly by the next teacher.

Many aspects of whole-school policy on recording achievement relate to assessment itself. For example, you and your colleagues may want to consider:

- How do teachers work with children to edit or correct work?
- Is there a consensus on issues such as writing on children's work?
- Is there agreement on the nature of appropriate feedback to children, and the place of descriptive comment or awarding 'scores'?

In making decisions about recording formats and approaches, schools need to consider both quality and manageability.

Your school needs to agree:

- What sort of records can be used which show what the children have experienced in terms of curriculum coverage as well as their attainment?
- How can attainment be recorded in those National Curriculum subject areas where statements of attainment relate to specific knowledge and competence? Are grids appropriate in these areas?
- How can descriptive comments relating to development be included? Any kind of tick box is inappropriate in those National Curriculum subjects in which statements of

attainment cover a broad spectrum of conceptual development and achievement.

- How can records incorporate the kinds of context in which children learn best?
- In what form should clear statements about children's learning needs be made?
- What are the best ways of summarising attainment at the end of a year?

Examples of approaches to recording

The following examples demonstrate the variety of strategies and formats which can be used as part of an agreed whole school approach. Whatever styles of recording are used, it is important for schools to monitor them and evaluate their usefulness.

- **brief contemporaneous notes of things observed**
  Some teachers keep a diary or journal in which to jot informal notes on significant happenings which occur spontaneously.

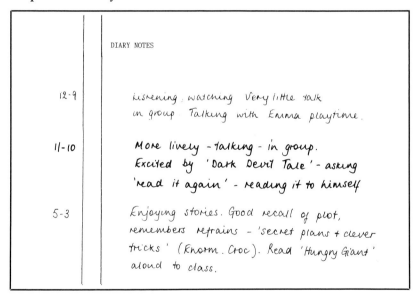

DIARY NOTES

12-9	Listening, watching Very little talk in group. Talking with Emma playtime.
11-10	More lively - talking - in group. Excited by 'Dark Devil Tale' - asking 'read it again' - reading it to himself
5-3	Enjoying stories. Good recall of plot, remembers refrains - 'secret plans + clever tricks' (Enorm. Croc). Read 'Hungry Giant' aloud to class.

Figure 26 *An infant teacher's diary notes on an individual child's literacy development.*

- **records of context**
  Important features of context which have a bearing on a child's achievement may arise quite unexpectedly and you may want to make informal notes about these. Other aspects can be planned, and the Primary Learning Record shows how you can use matrices effectively in planning and recording the context of assessments.

LEARNING CONTEXTS	SOCIAL CONTEXTS				
	individual	pair	small group	child with adult	small/large group with adult
language and literacy activities					
play, drama & story					
maths activities					
science activities					
design, construction, craft & art projects					
geographical activities					
historical activities					

From Talking and listening, Reading and Writing: diary of observations across the curriculum (in English and/or other community languages)

AREAS OF MATHEMATICS	SOCIAL CONTEXTS					
	individual	pair	small group	child with adult	small/large group with adult	
Using and applying maths						
Number inc measures						
Algebra						
Shape & space inc measures						
Data handling						

From Mathematics: diary of observations across the curriculum (in English and/or other community languages)

Figure 27 *(Reprinted from the* Primary Learning Record *by kind permission of the Centre for Language in Primary Education, Webber Row, London, SE1 8QW.)*

- **descriptive accounts**
  For recording some observations, you may want to describe in detail what children actually do and say, rather than to indicate to what extent pre-specified criteria have been met.

'N. became completely absorbed in role play with D and A. about 'Gem' TV series. Sometimes directing others ('you be', 'when I say... then you say'), also able to be directed (alright, I will), but generally in charge. Took on voice, mannerisms of part, completely unselfconscious. Directing others and very selective in who was allowed to take part. Rejected J. when she wanted to join in. Also writing about 'Gem' with group (B.A. and G.D.). All looking at Gem comic book, copying pictures (detail - eyelashes). Visual images having strong influence.

Figure 28 *More detailed descriptive comment by a teacher on an important aspect of one child's development.*

- **annotated work**

  Children's original written work, models, plans and
  diagrams can be retained in full or photographed and
  annotated by you or the child. However brief the comments,
  it is important that they are worthwhile and do not repeat
  information which can be obtained from a glance at the work
  itself. Some schools include provision for recording
  attainment against National Curriculum criteria.

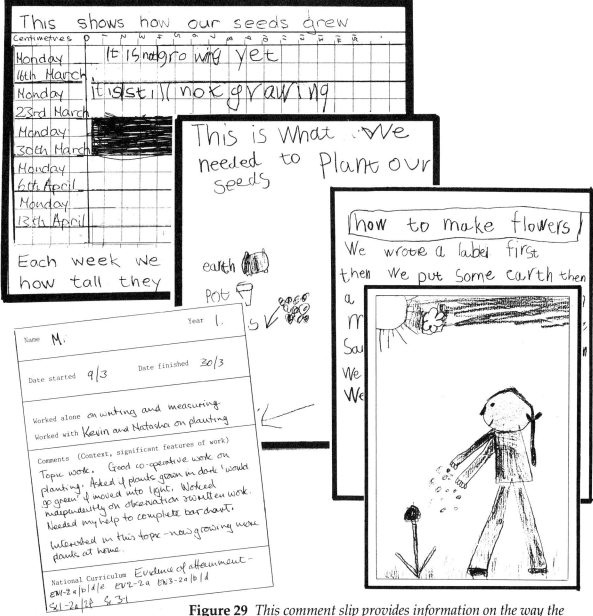

Figure 29 *This comment slip provides information on the way the
child went about the work and the help given by the teacher.*

- **specific detailed assessment by the teacher**
  Teachers may occasionally use specific diagnostic assessments with particular children, for example ILEA mathematics *Checkpoints* or reading miscue analyses.

Part Two: Running Record for *Tasha and the Wolf*	
Pages 2-5: Captions and signs ('Level 1 text')	

Page 2	Tasha ✓	the teacher ✓
Page 3	Tasha in the playground ✓ (WAY IN; SCHOOL)	dinner time ✓ (EXIT)
Page 4	the T picture of the wolf	Little Red Riding Hood ✓
Page 5	the school play ✓	(the end) ✓

Pages 6-11: 'Level 2 text'

Page 6	When Tasha came to her new school, she did not talk.
Page 7	She did not talk to her teacher, Miss White. She did not talk to the other children. She did not talk to anyone. Miss White <u>was</u>/sad. 'Tasha,' she said, 'Please try to talk.' But Tasha (just) (shut) her lips and said nothing.
Page 8	She said nothing in the classroom. She said nothing in the playground.
Page 9	She said nothing in the hall. At dinner time the children/talked so much that the dinner ladies had to shout. But Tasha just ate her dinner and said nothing.
Page 10	T After dinner the children in Tasha's class tried to make friends. 'Come and play ball with us, Tasha,' said Mark. He went over to Tasha and held out the ball. But Tasha did not (even) look at him. Mark put the ball in his pocket and walked away.
Page 11	Anna went over to Tasha. She put her hand on Tasha's arm and said 'You can be my best/friend if you like.' But Tasha just shut her lips and said nothing. Soon the other children gave up trying to make friends and left her alone.

Comments on fluency and expression

Generally good, some hesitation on page 10 - re-read first part and picked up well. Good fluent reading of speech passages - taking on 'voice' of speaker.

Figure 30 *An extract from a running record of a child's miscues. (From* Formative Assessment in the National Curriculum: Reading, *Hodder and Stoughton, 1991.)*

- **personal or group recording by children**
  Children can be encouraged to record using the same range
  of strategies as the teacher. For example, you can ask
  children to record against a set of criteria, write a descriptive
  account or brief annotation, or make a tape recording.

```
              Notes of your group's work

              Decide on one person in your group
           who will write down what you want to say.


Name of each person in the group




Describe what you had to do.  (Did you find out something,
plan something, write something together?)




What were you aiming to produce? (Was it a presentation to
the class, some art work, tape recordings, etc.?)




Explain how the group planned the work. (Did you talk, make
lists of ideas?)




What did each person in the group do?




What do you think have been the most interesting parts of
the work?



Date work started

Date work finished
```

Figure 31 *An example of the kind of format for group recording now
being developed by schools.*

- **grids and tick-sheets**

  Some National Curriculum subjects contain very specific statements of attainment which must be used as assessment criteria. It is important to keep an overview of class progress in these subjects. These statements of attainment can be organised so that you can mark off children's attainments. This kind of record can be kept on a single sheet for the whole class, or on separate sheets which can be put into individual children's profile folders.

  It is also important to have provision for making brief descriptive notes of important features of an individual child's work which fall outside particular criteria, and some formats provide for this.

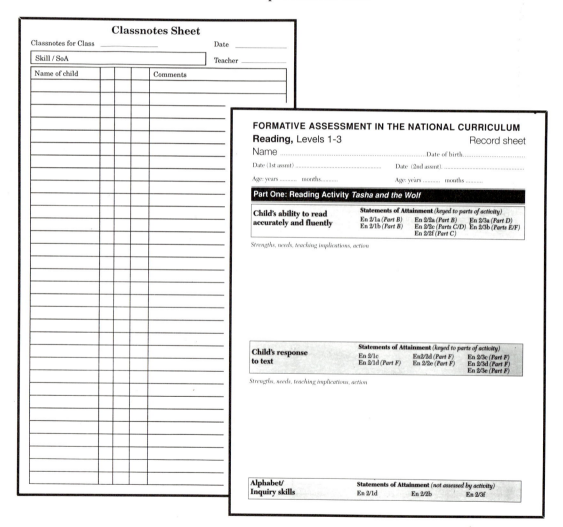

Figure 32 *The Classnotes Sheet is taken from the Primary Science Record and is reproduced by kind permission of teachers at the South London Science and Technology Centre. The Reading Record sheet is used in conjunction with the running record shown on page 72. It has provision for recording statements of attainment, making descriptive comment and forward planning.*

- **parental comments**
  Parents can provide a range of information and evidence. In many cases they already contribute to the recording of what children have read at home, and are increasingly becoming involved in supplying information and comment through parent–teacher conferences. You can also ask them to encourage their children to bring to school any evidence of interests and activities outside school, including involvement in community schools.

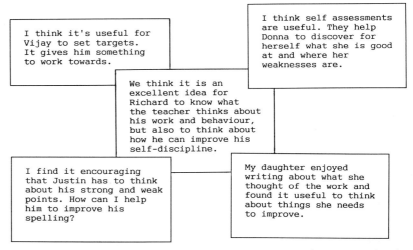

I think it's useful for Vijay to set targets. It gives him something to work towards.

I think self assessments are useful. They help Donna to discover for herself what she is good at and where her weaknesses are.

We think it is an excellent idea for Richard to know what the teacher thinks about his work and behaviour, but also to think about how he can improve his self-discipline.

I find it encouraging that Justin has to think about his strong and weak points. How can I help him to improve his spelling?

My daughter enjoyed writing about what she thought of the work and found it useful to think about things she needs to improve.

Figure 33 *Parents' comments on self-assessment and target setting by their children.*

School and classroom management issues

The management of approaches to planning and recording needs to begin from the school development plan and involve all staff, particularly in view of the need for coverage of the National Curriculum across Key Stages.

Suggestions for a programme of staff INSET on this aspect are made in Chapter 9.

What is feasible in individual classrooms is governed, to some extent, by class size. However, teachers need to explore all possible sources of support, particularly those for finding time for observing and recording individuals and small groups, and for conducting reviews with children.

You may want to consider:

- **using all available adult classroom support in keeping records**
  The contribution of Section 11 teachers and support teachers to record-keeping is very important; their insights on children's achievements and learning needs require recognition. Ancillary staff and parents working in the class can also provide factual evidence that supports your professional assessment.

● **developing children's independence and classroom responsibilities**

The most important contributors to the management of the classroom can be children themselves if they are expected and enabled to work responsibly and independently. Most teachers do not have significant classroom help, and can only free themselves to observe and record if children are self-sustaining in their work and assist with its recording.

From the time they enter school you can encourage children to:

–take control of their learning, in particular engaging with reading and writing in an independent and purposeful way;
appropriate ways;
–plan and work collaboratively in pairs and groups;
–use sources other than you, the teacher for support, for example, their peers, libraries and computers;
–take responsibility for the management of classroom resources.

Figure 34 shows one teacher's lesson plan for a writing workshop session with a whole class of Year 5 children, which was intended to promote a high quality of writing and group support for sustained independent work.

```
Teacher initiates class discussion on creative writing.
Teacher also takes part.

Children work in pairs. Each child is asked to write down,
independently, two different ideas for a piece of imaginative
writing.
Teacher writes down her ideas.

Teacher institutes a short period of discussion between pairs.
Which idea looks most promising, and why?

A class sharing session takes place. Some children try out their
ideas and get opinions from a wider group of their peers.
Teacher shares her ideas too, and notes any significant comments
by individual children.

Children and teacher decide independently on a subject and write
alternative openings.

Teacher institutes a short period of discussion of openings
between pairs.

Class sharing session. Children read aloud their alternative
openings and explain ideas. Class discuss the effect of the
different openings on the audience.
Teacher takes part. She notes any significant comments.


The opportunities for writing and on-going discussion in pairs
gradually become longer, with class sharing at intervals judged
necessary by the teacher.
```

Figure 34 *The sharing of ideas at the beginning of the activity supported children, gave them the broadest possible stimulation and a sense of purpose and audience. The carefully fostered pair-work provided a basis for continued support. This careful planning both promoted a high quality of writing and freed the teacher at a later stage to observe, talk with individual children for extended periods and make detailed records.*

9
Developing school policy on records of achievement

Areas relating to policy

Figure 35 details the main areas that need consideration in the development of a whole-school approach to assessment, recording and reporting.

Suggestions for a programme of INSET

Preparing

All staff should have time to consider the processes underlying primary records of achievement and to reflect on ways in which these processes can be developed in the school to meet existing needs. Using the guide, staff (perhaps in pairs) can be asked to choose and think about:

- a particular chapter;
- a specific area, for example involving parents or liaising with other teachers and schools;
- the range of examples provided.

Whilst preparing in this way, staff also need to think about:

- existing practice in the school;
- the relationship between existing practice and the principles and processes which underlie records of achievement;
- priority areas for developing school policy.

Staff should each prepare a short report of findings and issues and present this at the first INSET session. The information provided by these reports can form the basis for planning.

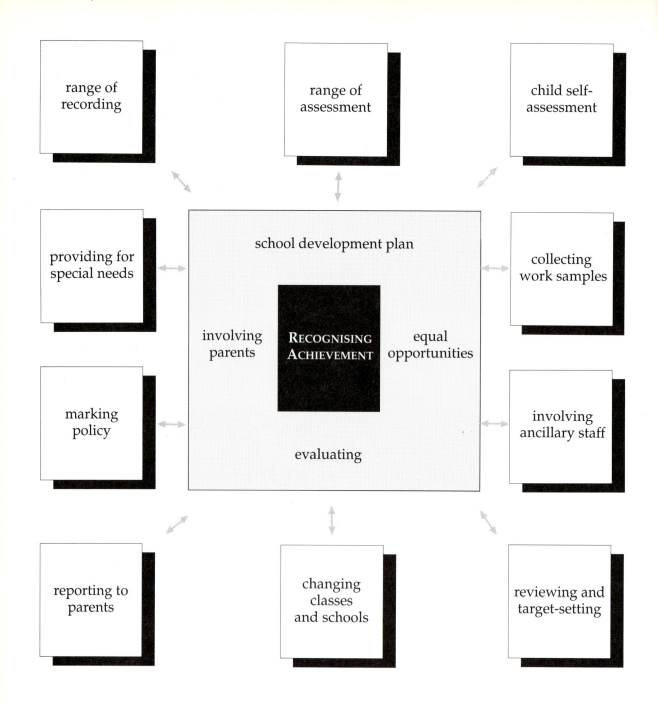

range of recording

range of assessment

child self-assessment

providing for special needs

school development plan

involving parents

RECOGNISING ACHIEVEMENT

equal opportunities

collecting work samples

marking policy

involving ancillary staff

evaluating

reporting to parents

changing classes and schools

reviewing and target-setting

RECOGNISING ACHIEVEMENT
Curriculum planning, assessment and recording which recognises achievement in all areas of development, enables individual children to achieve and progress in a broad and balanced way.

SCHOOL DEVELOPMENT PLAN
The school development plan is the starting point for any initiative to develop policy on assessment, recording and reporting. It enables staff to budget for appropriate finance and to allocate time and resources for development. The plan also provides the framework for taking decisions relating to staff involvement, identifying priorities for development and evaluating progress.

Involving parents

Plans should be made to involve parents in recognising and recording children's achievement. Parents can contribute to:

- early years' records;
- induction activities;
- portfolios;
- classroom activities;
- parents' meetings;
- family assemblies;
- parent conferences;
- school reports and records.

Equal opportunities

A school policy on equality of opportunity should set out details of ways in which staff can maintain high expectations and ensure access to the whole curriculum for all children.

Evaluating

Time for evaluating developments, both during and at the end of the year, needs to be incorporated into initial planning.

Range of recording

Agreement is needed on suitable methods for recording all talents and skills – for example languages understood, spoken and written by bilingual children.

This provides opportunities to gather evidence of achievement within and beyond the National Curriculum and activities outside school.

Range of assessment

The use of a range of strategies for assessment, including informal observations by the teacher, presentations and demonstrations by the children and reviews of products – for example, written work and diagrams.

Child self-assessment

Details of support for children and opportunities for self-assessment can include:

- annotating work;
- writing personal statements;
- keeping logs of work;
- keeping details of interests.

This provides opportunities to:

- *involve children in record-keeping;*
- *help the teacher gather evidence for assessment and record-keeping;*
- *establish clear links with statements of attainment which relate to self-assessment.*

Providing for special needs

This requires establishing:

- mechanisms to identify children's particular needs;

- procedures for observing, diagnosing, intervening and noting strategies employed;
- clear policy on reviewing and the involvement of outside agencies.

This provides opportunities for diagnostic and formative assessment.

Collecting work samples

Agreement is needed on:

- the quantity of work samples to be retained;
- the methods and criteria for selection.

This provides opportunities to gather hard evidence for assessment of all-round development, including progress in National Curriculum subjects, to inform planning and build the records of achievement.

Marking policy

There should be agreed purposes and methods used for day-to-day recorded feedback to children so that achievements are recognised and needs identified.

This provides staff with opportunities to develop consistent ways of responding to children.

Involving ancillary staff

The ways in which ancillary staff can be involved and trained in observing and recording what children say and do, need to be established.

This provides assistance to teachers in the gathering of evidence.

Reporting to parents

Details need to be clarified as to the format, contents and timing of reports which meet legal requirements and the needs of children, parents and receiving teachers.

This provides opportunities to ensure continuity for the child, inform and involve parents, and demonstrate the work and expertise of the school.

Changing classes and schools

A process needs to exist for the transfer of records between classes and schools which presents receiving teachers with a clear picture of individual achievement on which to build.

This promotes greater continuity of recording and assessment across the whole curriculum, including National Curriculum levels of attainment.

Reviewing and target-setting

Planned provision of time within the curriculum for reviewing progress and setting targets with children is required.

This provides opportunities to use assessment formatively.

Figure 35 *Developing school policy on assessment, recording and reporting*

Structuring a programme for INSET

One way in which development might be undertaken is suggested in the following programme, but the number of INSET sessions needed to plan and implement the whole school policy will vary.

Session 1
Reports are presented by staff on aspects of primary records of achievement.

Session 2
Consideration is given to primary records of achievement in relation to the school development plan.
    Within this context staff can:

- identify and agree the priority areas for development;
- consider implications for their own professional development;
- estimate the time required for further INSET and support;
- agree realistic short- and long-term developments;
- decide which members of staff should initially be involved.

Session 3
Plan the details of development in the school.
Staff:

- set short-term objectives:
  Example One: Completion of one self-assessment in one curriculum area by all Year 6 children during the first term;
  Example Two: Brief report back to staff at end of first term by all teachers involved in development;
- set long-term objectives:
  Example: Implementation of self-assessment and review procedures across Year 6 curriculum by the end of the year.

Session 4
Plan the evaluation of development.
    Time needs to be set aside for staff to evaluate progress to date. Time may be used for:

- reviewing the processes undertaken and the development of recording which has taken place;
- reviewing whole-school policy in relation to the school development plan.